RESTORED AMERICA

RESTORED AMERICA

by Deirdre Stanforth

photographed by Louis Reens

Praeger Publishers, New York

Published in the United States of America in 1975
by Praeger Publishers, Inc.
111 Fourth Avenue, New York, N.Y. 10003

Library of Congress Cataloging in Publication
   Data

Stanforth, Deirdre.
   Restored America.

   1. Historic buildings—United States—Conservation and restoration. I. Reens, Louis, joint
author. II. Title.
E159.S72   069'.53   74-5573
ISBN 0-275-49740-2

Designed by Joseph Bourke Del Valle

Frontispiece: Restored drawing room, Lafayette
   Park, St. Louis, Missouri (page 88).

Printed in the United States of America

Contents ❧

II Adaptive Use   159

Conversion to Private Use

Conversion to Public and Commercial Use

Organizations   245

Picture Credits   246

America is being rediscovered. Many of us, spurred by the upcoming Bicentennial, are actively seeking our roots. We feel the need to relate our past to the present and then to look ahead, to plan an even better future; so we are searching, and we are finding many things.

This spirit of rediscovery is evident in many areas. New research, based on old documents read with a new perspective, has produced a score of publications and articles on various aspects of the American past. Decorative arts and finely crafted furnishings that were discarded over the years for a more modern look are now avidly sought, for "investment" as well as for pleasure. Reproductions of varying quality and commemorative items, celebrating the free-enterprise system, are sold to a public eager to be and have a part of "history." We are even taking a new look at the land itself, and recognizing that natural resources are not limitless. In short, we are not just reconsidering and gaining a new appreciation of the intangible heritage of ideas and traditions that have become the essence of America; we are also finding and learning to value the tangible treasures that have been buried by years of neglect and indifference.

Unlike the land, which nature can eventually reclaim, the buildings that make up America and give us a sense of where we are physically and historically are irreplaceable. As a nation, we are coming to realize that the places where our predecessors lived, worked, and played are special. They are different. They can reveal the past to us in a way that words cannot, and if allowed to survive, they can enrich our lives and those of our children.

Some of these buildings, generally houses, have withstood the pressures of time and have been maintained and used for the purpose for which they were constructed. These are showpieces of preservation. They exemplify the credo espoused by the National Trust for Historic Preservation and other preservation organizations: "It is better to preserve than repair, better to repair than restore, better to restore than reconstruct."

Unfortunately, most structures of the past were not maintained and preserved. Many were not repaired. A large number were either replaced in the name of progress, abandoned and left to the elements, or degraded by inappropriate modernization. It is this group of buildings that provided the raw materials for the restoration projects featured in this book. As the examples indicate, some buildings can be restored to their previous uses; others must be saved by adapting them to new uses consistent with contemporary needs. Inner-city houses can again accommodate families; art students can learn painting and sculpting techniques in bypassed railroad stations; mills can become apartments with a character all their own. Historic-preservation organizations can even move into cemetery waiting stations! The reuse of our architecture is limited generally by local zoning ordinances, legal standards for security, financial resources—and our imaginations.

Those who undertake the restoration of a building must be prepared, however, to face cynics who will ask, "Why bother?" The answer to this challenge will be different for each situation. Some preservationists are motivated by a respect for their heritage and the desire to pass it on to future generations. Others view preservation as one facet of the protection of the total environment. A few are reacting to the wastefulness of modern society. They see still useful materials being thoughtlessly discarded, and energy—human and mechanical—being needlessly expended. Still others, who are aware of the economic benefits of preservation, view it as an investment. No matter what the answer, the important point is that the historic-preservation movement is achieving its goal. Preservationists are convincing their fellow Americans that saving our heritage is not a nostalgic escape but a meaningful activity for today and an essential task for tomorrow.

The National Trust for Historic Preservation is proud to be a part of the preservation community. When it was chartered by Congress in 1949 as a private, nonprofit organization with the responsibility of encouraging public participation in the preservation of sites, buildings, and objects significant in American history and culture, the road ahead seemed long and was unknown. But, since that time, the Trust has grown from a handful of members to more than 75,000 individual members and 1,300 member organizations, representing hundreds of thousands more.

In addition to encouraging others to act, the Trust as the national private leader in preservation has assisted in setting standards. As the owner of more than a dozen historic properties, it seeks to be an example of quality maintenance, restoration, research, and interpretation. From its headquarters in Washington, D.C., and its field offices, the Trust offers preservationists a variety of services—professional consultation, publications, financial aid, meetings and conferences, reference and research assistance, interesting educational tours, and information on opportunities for education and employment in the preservation field.

In this work, the Trust is not alone. Hundreds of local preservation organizations labor daily to save their communities. State organizations focus on planning for preservation and on solving problems common to many cities and towns in the states. Government, too, plays a role. With the passage of the National Historic Preservation Act of 1966, the federal government officially committed itself to a policy of federal support of preservation. Over the years, it has given preservation increasing support, and federal agencies now are required to consider preservation concerns when planning their activities. State and local governments have likewise become partners in the preservation movement. Everywhere, officials recognize that citizens care about the appearance of their communities.

All of this activity and cooperation portend a bright future for America's cultural heritage. But there are still problems to be solved and buildings to be rescued. How do we preserve an area without disrupting established neighborhoods? Can tax burdens be equitably distributed so that older structures are not penalized because of their fortuitous locations or circumstances of technology?

There are solutions to these problems, but finding them will require many people— people like those mentioned in this book and those who read it—working together. The time to restore America is today; in fact, the time was yesterday and it will also be tomorrow.

James Biddle
President
National Trust for Historic Preservation

Acknowledgments ❧

This book would not have been possible without the help and cooperation of the people whose names are mentioned in the text, as well as those who preferred to remain anonymous. We would like to express our sincere appreciation and heartfelt thanks to all of them, and to the many others, listed below, whose assistance was invaluable.

Louis O. Gropp, Editor, House and Garden Guides; Terry Morton, National Trust for Historic Preservation; Mrs. Lawrence Adams, Mrs. Waldo P. Lambdin, and Mrs. Richard A. Campbell, Natchez; Mary Wharton, Newport; Mrs. S. Henry Edmunds and Alicia Rudolf, Charleston; Beth Lattimore, Savannah; John J. Collins, Marshall; Jacob Schmitt, Schenectady; Judith Waldhorn, San Francisco; Mary Means, National Trust Midwest Office; Lawrence D. Glass, Chicago; Carolyn Pitts, Cape May; William Hague, Key West; Charles Eilerman, Covington; Ronald Neely, Georgetown, Colorado; Robertson E. Collins, Jacksonville, Oregon; Barbara and Bob Reich and Dudley Brown, Washington; Stephanie Churchill, Sam Weller, and Milton Weilenman, Salt Lake City; Frederic L. Chase, Jr., Providence; Denys Peter Myers, Alexandria; Mr. and Mrs. C. Franklin Brown, Galena; Steven Raiche, Connecticut; Nancy N. Holmes and Mrs. Hamp Uzzelle, Mobile; Peggy Armitage, Portsmouth; Richard Bradford, Santa Fe; Mrs. Wyatt French, Betty Moore, Thomas Adams, and Dean Levi, Richmond; Mrs. Winfield Scott Hamlin, San Antonio; Louis Sporl, Mary Morrison, Martha Robinson, Myrlin McCullar, Eugene Cizek, and David Sigle, New Orleans; Louis Singer, Brooklyn; Mrs. Barham Gary, Annapolis; Earle Shettleworth, Jr., Maine; Lucille Basler, Ste. Genevieve; Sally Iliff, Baltimore; and Axel Grosser, who printed the photographs.

We are also grateful to our editor, Brenda Gilchrist, who conceived the idea for this book and followed it through to completion with unstinting care and devotion, assisted by Ellyn Childs and Harriet Bee.

Deirdre Stanforth
Louis Reens

I Restored Houses &

Introduction

After two hundred years as a nation, we are at last beginning to place some value on our own history. A wave of nostalgia is sweeping America, awakening us to the fact that we have been destroying the very sense of permanence that we now crave. Our perpetual passion for anything new at the sacrifice of whatever stands in the way, is coming to be recognized as prodigal wastefulness. We have learned that there is a limit to our resources, an end to our frontiers. Replacing a Greek revival mansion with a gasoline station is no longer universally accepted as a sign of progress.

Many Americans travel to Europe to enjoy an ambience derived from visible evidence of the past, but few relate the experience to their own country. What if the Romans had demolished the Forum and Colosseum to make way for office buildings? If they had been as devoted to progress as we are, Rome, Florence, and Venice might look just like New York or Chicago. Since they insist on sacrificing so many acres of valuable real estate to ancient monuments, why do they leave all those stones and broken columns lying about? Americans would have reconstructed them (eradicating their authenticity), so that tourists could see what those buildings really looked like!

Thanks to cycles of fashion and the value of real estate, we have been razing and rebuilding our cities since at least the eighteenth century. Boston has so little evidence of the important events that took place in the Cradle of Liberty that the visitor must often be satisfied with "This was the site of . . ." All trace of New York's Dutch settlers has long since vanished; to most Americans, they are not even a memory. Where is there any reminder of the bloody battles that raged across Long Island and Brooklyn when Washington retreated from the British, while our nation's future hung in the balance?

In nineteenth-century Manhattan, entire lavishly built neighborhoods were constructed and wiped out within a decade. The remaining half of one such splendid block, Colonnade Row (home of Franklin D. Roosevelt's grandfather, Astors, and Vanderbilts) stands tragically crumbling, unnoticed, on Lafayette Street. Even George Washington's home, Mount Vernon, was neglected for many years. The charming brick houses of William Penn's colonial followers, surrounding Independence Hall, distintegrated into a slum that was nearly bulldozed into oblivion before it was rescued for restoration in 1959. And directly behind the Capitol of the United States, the dwellings of our early senators and congressmen became Washington's most run-down neighborhood until restoration began in the 1950s. These are only a few of many houses, redolent with history, that were nearly lost; many more are gone forever.

Fine buildings continue to be destroyed for parking lots, highways, apartment and office buildings, and motels. But people are beginning to object. They are searching for their roots, something to build on, something in which they can take pride. Young people, particularly, are reacting against the plastic society, the emptiness, lack of character, and solidity of suburbia, the sameness of apartments and developments. They are coming back into the cities to find, under layers of filth, the fine homes their ancestors deserted decades ago. They are peeling back linoleum from parquet floors, releasing mahogany shutters and sliding doors that were nailed up into walls when capricious fashion shunned them, stripping caked enamel off carved woodwork and bronze hardware, and repairing insets of etched and stained glass. Some of these young people are taking great pains to restore carefully and authentically. It is a labor of love and pride.

Though many fine old houses can be found in the country and in small towns, the majority are in the population centers, because that is where early settlers congregated. Merchants, craftsmen, and bankers all built their homes near the town hall, church, and stores, for con-

Saltbox house, Guilford, Connecticut (opposite)

venience and safety. As industry, noise, and dirt increased, so did facility of transportation, and it became easy and fashionable to move out of town. The automobile made it so easy that cities were almost completely abandoned as places to live, except by the poor, who did not have any choice. They found shelter in those splendid homes that were left behind, but dozens of people were crowded into one or two rooms, and town houses became slums.

Many acres of these houses were wiped out under misguided urban renewal programs during the 1950s, but fortunately, many still remain in most cities. Wholesale demolition was halted in the late 1950s and early 1960s, and combined with restoration in Portsmouth, New Hampshire; New Haven, Connecticut; New York City; and Philadelphia. Results began to show that old houses could be adapted for contemporary living within any taste or life-style. They made homes as good as anything built today, or better, providing amenities like front doors, gardens, human scale, individuality, and a sense of neighborhood. A spontaneous surge of restoration activity has taken place all over America and has given a tremendous boost to dying cities, as well as to the preservation of our architectural heritage.

Since affluence caused our wastefulness, one great source of architectural wealth is in cities that suffered financial reverses and simply could not afford the building booms that wiped out earlier structures. Charleston, South Carolina, Savannah, Georgia, and Natchez, Mississippi, were all fantastically wealthy prior to the Civil War and destitute afterward. Some towns, whose prosperity depended on a river, were left high and dry by fortune when the river either changed course or silted up, as it did in Galena, Illinois. Others, like Marshall, Michigan (page 21), and Jacksonville, Oregon, were bypassed by the railroads. Western mining towns that were created overnight were abandoned overnight. They were centers of unparalleled prosperity until the Sherman Silver Act was repealed in 1893. Populations vanished; homes, hotels, opera houses, and stores were deserted. Mrs. Walter Paepcke, who, with her husband, rediscovered Aspen, Colorado, in the mid-1940s, recalls finding only three people on the main street at eleven in the morning, all drunk. There were snow drifts in the corridors of the Hotel Jerome, and none of the wooden houses had been painted in fifty years. Today those same houses (the type that are considered expendable all over America) are so highly valued that they sell for prices as high as New York City town houses. Thanks to the Paepckes' restoration efforts, installation of a ski lift, and foundation of a humanities and arts center, Aspen is a boom town again, forced to declare a moratorium on new building that has nearly smothered its Victorian character. Nearby Georgetown, Colorado, another mining ghost town just awakened from a long sleep, is determined to avoid Aspen's mistakes and maintains firm control of its architectural integrity.

The West is at last realizing that it has its own special character, even if it is not as old as the East. Denver, finding acres of its center flattened for urban renewal, organized Historic Denver, Inc., in 1970. Making up for lost time, the organization restored the Molly Brown house, rescued and adapted to new use the old cable car barn, began an ambitious plan to incorporate the remainder of its earliest settlement, Auraria, into a new college campus, and published a book called Historic Denver—all within three years.

Aroused, middle and western America have become more active and enthusiastic than the East, where old houses are taken for granted. Old neighborhoods are being revived in St. Paul, Minnesota; Raleigh, North Carolina; and Dallas, Texas. Lafayette Square in St. Louis has made amazing progress in five years. The neighborhood was considered dangerous, and much of it was condemned, but now houses are purchased within a day or two after they go on the market, and house tours attract ten thousand people.

It is obvious that Americans are becoming increasingly interested in preservation, which

used to be associated only with little old ladies who wanted to petrify the past in dry, dusty museums. We needed the museums; we still do. But now preservation is coming alive. People want to live in those houses, not just look at them. And that is as it should be. Buildings ought to be put back to work, to serve a living function, as they were always meant to.

Preservation, restoration, reconstruction, renovation, and remodeling; these words are so often confused that a definition of terms is in order. The last two involve changing the basic structure or design of a building. If buildings have no interior detail worth saving, they are often remodeled by gutting and redesigning the space in dramatic contemporary style. When buildings that have fine interiors are used in this manner, it is almost as destructive as total demolition, but when they have not, it can be an excellent re-use. As long as exteriors are retained or restored to harmonize with surrounding buildings, this type of renovation is entirely in keeping with the finest historic district.

Preservation means keeping something the way it always was; restoration means putting it back into its original condition. Reconstruction, or reproduction, means remaking, or copying in new materials. One building can contain elements of all three. There is a tendency to confuse restoration and reconstruction; Williamsburg, Virginia, is referred to as a restoration, whereas it is primarily a reconstruction. The danger in encouraging this misuse of words is that people will no longer know how to distinguish between a copy and the real thing. It might be compared to making no distinction between a reupholstered antique and a reproduction.

To follow the same analogy, a perfectly preserved antique is clearly preferable to one that needs restoration, but it will also be rarer and more costly. We have all heard about discovering battered, dusty furniture, blackened paintings, or scorned Tiffany lamps in the attic, and learning that they were valuable. The same applies to old houses. There are many thousands of them standing unrecognized and neglected all over America, waiting to be rediscovered.

How literally should we interpret "restoration"? Obviously it is impractical to restore a house entirely authentically and live in it. Even museums require bathrooms, light, and heat. Not even a purist is willing to settle for an outhouse, wood stove, and gaslight.

Certainly exteriors should be treated as authentically as possible, for they affect many other people. An error in taste or judgment can have a deleterious effect on a block or an entire neighborhood. The exterior of a saltbox house of 1710 in Guilford, Connecticut, shown here (page 14) is an example of restoration at its best. Bright, garish colors, removal of integral design elements, such as cornices, changing size or style of windows or doors, adding raw aluminum storm windows or protruding air conditioners should be avoided.

As for interiors, we must begin by admitting the necessity of plumbing, wiring, heating, perhaps air conditioning, contemporary kitchens, and bathrooms. The rest is a matter of good taste and judicious compromise. Restoration, like marriage, should never be done in haste; there is equal opportunity to repent at leisure. The most successful restorations are done slowly, so that there is time to understand the building's character and integrity, and perhaps do some research into the history of the house and others like it. Why should one attempt to restore authentically? Because, if for no other reason, it simply looks better. The integrity of a house can be distorted or destroyed if its original floor plan, proportions, or salient characteristics are altered. Small rooms look wrong with large mantels, Victorian houses look dreadful with colonial multipaned doors and windows, eighteenth-century floors that were meant to be painted look raw and naked if they are scraped bare, and any period house looks ghastly with Celotex ceilings.

Of course, one does not have to live with the colors or wallpapers chosen by eighteenth-

Saltbox house, Guilford, Connecticut (opposite)

or nineteenth-century owners, but it would be advisable to try, as much as possible, to retain the original feeling. If one goes too far with drastic changes, the effect can be jarring. If it is necessary to scrape a painted floor, it should at least be stained dark.

There is often a temptation to overrestore; but there is no point in buying an old house to make it look new. So much can be lost if its character is erased by the removal of every nick in the woodwork, every bump and crack in the plaster. The same effect would be achieved by sanding and varnishing an antique. Architects and contractors, usually preferring to rip out old material and replace it with new, can do irreparable damage. Owners must be hardheaded and vigilant in preventing this professional vandalism.

How far back should one go in restoring a building to its original period, when it has accumulated layers of taste in its evolving history as a home? There is no standard answer. If we consider asbestos siding, Permastone, or flush doors degrading to a nineteenth-century house, is not Victorianization of an eighteenth-century house equally offensive? Yes and no. It can be a dreadful mistake to rip out handsomely designed later details if they are well done and the scale is suitable. To make a concrete illustration: a fifteenth-century Irish castle was remodeled in the Georgian period with wood floors and paneling, and with fluted columns around its Gothic windows. Certainly this fine woodwork should not be discarded in the name of authenticity in order to strip back to the original stone walls? In the case of the Tarrytown, New York, "restoration" of Philipsburg Manor, a house that evolved in three distinct sections, representing three periods of taste, was demolished down to the one original wall of the earliest part of the building and reconstructed to that period. The two later additions were stripped off, and there is virtually nothing real remaining.

Why restore? In some cases, it is less expensive to rehabilitate an old house than to build a new one, depending on its condition. But often restoration is not only more costly, but more difficult. Even when a house has been carefully examined by a building inspector, there may be unknown problems lurking beneath walls and floors. Replacement of parts that are either not standard or no longer available adds to the difficulty and expense. However, aside from the satisfaction, which is priceless, a well-restored house may appreciate in value, as an antique does. In fact, if it happens to be in a run-down neighborhood, it can be the finest investment opportunity conceivable, and possibly double or triple in value.

As to the question "Why restore?" in a broader context, the benefits have been clearly and unequivocally proved so many times that it is difficult to understand why city officials and bankers must be convinced again and again. Many impressive statistics are available to prove the economic benefits of restoration. New Orleans's Vieux Carré not only attracts many millions of tourist and convention dollars, it also provides permanent stability to the downtown area, encouraging businesses to locate there. The Vieux Carré was a slum prior to the 1930s, when its charming old houses were restored by individuals who wanted to live in the city. The same story was repeated in Washington's Georgetown and New York's Greenwich Village. Yet a long, uphill battle was required to convince the civic and business leaders of Savannah, Georgia, that restoration, rather than demolition and modernization, would bring businesses and residents back to their city. It not only did that, but attracted significant tourist income as well, in effect putting Savannah back on the map.

Why, in spite of these unquestioned successes, plus a long list of others, must the value of restoration be proved over and over again? Why are citizens, bankers, and government officials always skeptical and unable to relate these examples to their own cities? Why, with the highly profitable Vieux Carré under its very nose, has the city of New Orleans destroyed acres of equally valuable old houses in the past five years?

House, Marshall, Michigan

None of the above-mentioned restorations was achieved through civic or committee action. They were all brought about by individuals who wanted to live there, regardless of financial obstacles and municipal indifference. Georgetown, Greenwich Village, the Vieux Carré were all discovered and restored by people looking for inexpensive living space in the years following the Depression. In Georgetown, they were young people who came to work in Washington for Franklin D. Roosevelt's administration. In the Vieux Carré and Greenwich Village, they were artists and writers, willing to live in bohemian style, who would dwell in neighborhoods that respectable people spurned. As neighborhoods improve, prices always rise and the artists and writers are forced to look elsewhere. This pattern has been repeated in Old Town, Chicago, and SoHo and Brooklyn Heights in New York City. Courageous individuals have also led the way in the revival of Boston's South End; German Village, Columbus, Ohio; and Newport and Providence, Rhode Island—among many others.

Most of us have gotten into the habit of looking at buildings without actually seeing them. It becomes even harder to recognize intrinsic quality and potential value when the basic structure is concealed under artificial siding and cobbled-on additions, as well as filth and neglect. The opportunity to see that beauty uncovered again, and its potential realized, may encourage restoration of the many buildings that need it so very badly. May the success stories shown herein inspire countless imitators.

Chadds Ford, Pennsylvania

Abandoned for thirty-five years, this marvelous old stone house (2) was lucky enough to be brought back to life by people who appreciated its basic beauty and understood the value of restraint in restoration (3, 4). "There is no point in restoring an old house if you are going to make it look like new," says owner George Weymouth. Weymouth and his wife, Ann, are both natives of Brandywine Valley, where their house stands. The front part of the ground floor was built around 1683, probably as a trading post, after William Penn bought the land from the Lenape Indians. The remainder of the manor was built onto the original structure in about 1763 by a Scottish captain of the Royal Engineers, as a summer refuge from the heat of Philadelphia for himself and his mistress. Washington and Lafayette met at Point Lookout, just above the house, on the way to the crucial Battle of Brandywine, the defeat that preceded the victory at Valley Forge.

Following a colorful history, during which the property housed a powder mill, a grist mill, and then an iron foundry, it was last used by tenant farmers before it was abandoned to the elements and the cows that roamed through the ground floor. In 1961, the Weymouths bought the doorless, windowless shell (1). Nothing new has been put into the house except electricity, plumbing, kitchen, and baths. The old floors were patched with wood from other old buildings on the property, and, although all the mantels, save one, had been pulled off, they were found lying about the grounds. An original swing-out crane was found walled up in a fireplace. The missing hardware was replaced with Early American pieces (5; color, page 17).

This restoration is not unique in this lovely corner of Pennsylvania. Mr. Weymouth, a painter, is president of the Tri-County Conservancy and the Brandywine River Museum. The Conservancy was founded by Weymouth to further preservation, conservation, and restoration of the land in its natural condition. The museum is a fine example of adaptive use—an 1864 grist mill bought by Mr. Weymouth in 1967 and converted to a museum dedicated to the art of the area. Four generations of artists have lived and worked in the valley at Chadds Ford— Howard Pyle and three generations of Wyeths. Ann Weymouth is N. C. Wyeth's granddaughter, Andrew's niece. The Andrew Wyeths have restored a similar house, as well as an old mill that now serves as an office.

1

3

4

Santa Fe, founded in 1610, may be the oldest city in America. Its citizens call it "the city different," and it is indeed unique in many ways that should serve as examples to other cities. Santa Fe has remained stubbornly and steadfastly proud of its character and determined to retain it in spite of progress, free enterprise, and the lure of the almighty dollar. It may well be the only city in America of almost unadulterated architectural unity. Hotels, offices, and stores are all built in the style originated by Indians and Spanish settlers from indigenous natural materials. Though Santa Fe has enchanted tourists with the foreign flavor of its ubiquitous milk-chocolate-colored adobe buildings, it has not allowed the ye-olde-shoppe syndrome to prevail. Nor has it followed the policy of New Orleans, where Vieux Carré residents and neighborhood businesses are sacrificed in favor of tourism.

Seldom have Santa Fe residents abandoned their old buildings or allowed them to deteriorate. For more than three and a half centuries, buildings have been constantly re-used, evolving and growing as they are restored. While the majority of Americans have had no respect for their past, repeatedly discarding their architectural heritage, the people of Santa Fe have revered theirs.

Here, where there is respect for the evolution of architecture as living history, one would never find the kind of restoration that strips a building down to its earliest nucleus to create an artificial historic display. On the contrary, the Historical Santa Fe Foundation has placed plaques on some of its modified adobes, its few Victorian houses, and nonconforming public buildings, although its historic district ordinance compels all new buildings to comply with the adobe style.

On the other hand, some think that these controls restrict the natural growth of architectural style. There is a feeling, even among preservationists, that architects must be given creative freedom to change with the times. The prevailing opinion is that new buildings should not be indistinguishable from old ones, and that in a historic district, they should only be required to harmonize with earlier structures in terms of size, color, texture, and rhythm of door and window openings. Some also quarrel with the validity of continuing to use mud as a building material. In fact, when George Romney

was Secretary of Housing, an edict was issued declaring that adobe would no longer be recognized as a legal building material. The order was rescinded following a New Mexican protest pointing out that the five-story Taos Pueblo (surely the world's oldest apartment building) erected in the tenth century, was still in use.

But it is the material and method of use that produced the style. Although imitation adobes were built of cinder blocks in the 1950s, the 1960s saw a return to the original mud bricks. "Puddled adobe" was the earliest means of building with mud. Indians simply built up the mud in layers, much as a primitive clay pot is constructed without the use of a potter's wheel. The Spanish, arriving in the seventeenth century, introduced the method of forming the mud into bricks. The handmade, sun-baked bricks were assembled and mortared with mud, and the surface was plastered with mud. Poor families can still repair their houses with nature's materials, which helps explain the absence of slums in Santa Fe. Flat roofs were made of pine logs called vigas, spaced about thirty inches apart (and often protruding through the front of the house), with smaller aspen poles, *lattias,* laid crosswise or diagonally over the vigas. Next came a layer of twigs or brush, topped with eighteen inches of dirt. Floors, originally made of dirt hardened with ox blood, were laid with glazed brick.

Today, houses are still built in the same manner, except that more permanent, adobe-colored cement stucco has replaced mud plaster. Roofs are now insulated with pumice rather than brush, and covered with roofing felt and a layer of hot asphalt topped with gravel. The earliest houses had walls three to four feet thick, with small window openings for security, and to keep houses warm in winter and cool in summer. Walls became thinner as danger lessened, and by the 1820s, they had become more or less standardized at twenty-four inches.

Following the end of Spanish rule, when New Mexico became an American territory, new materials came in from the north via the Santa Fe Trail. The Territorial style resulted: handmade, rough-hewn post and corbels, windows and doors were replaced with millwork doors, double-hung sashes, and slender, square porch columns, all painted white, or sometimes sky blue. Cement, stucco, and lime were introduced to replace mud plaster, and fired bricks were

used to trim and protect the rims of adobe parapets on the roofs of houses.

The basic adobe style, and its Territorial modifications are the only types of design for new buildings acceptable to the architectural review board of the Old Santa Fe Association. The Association was formed in 1926, "to preserve and maintain the ancient landmarks, historical structures and traditions of Old Santa Fe, to guide its growth and development in such a way as to sacrifice as little as possible of that unique charm born of age, tradition and environment which are the priceless assets and heritage of Old Santa Fe."

An historic district ordinance was enacted in 1957, when a historic building was demolished at night to make way for a parking lot. The ordinance has since been tested and upheld as constitutional by the New Mexico Supreme Court. However, the Old Santa Fe Association has had to remain constantly vigilant and ready to fight to enforce the ordinance in order to preserve their town's collective façade. Recently, they rescued a building from destruction by Howard Johnson's, which wanted to build on the site, and they have fought Holiday Inn and others over the size and conspicuousness of their signs. The ordinance also limits the size of plate-glass windows. The downtowns of most American cities illustrate the benefit of such restrictions.

Cerrillos Road, the route into town from the south, is outside the jurisdiction of the ordinance. Driving into Santa Fe on this all-too-typical highway, lined with the garish eyesores that Americans have come to take for granted, one sees what our country has become, as opposed to what it could be.

The handsome house shown here (6, 8) is a fine example of an early adobe that has been almost continuously lived in since it was built about 1700. Though it has grown larger through additions by successive owners, its earliest rooms have been carefully preserved.

Journals written between 1720 and 1730 refer to a grist mill on the site, and indeed, foundations of the original mill building and evidence of the undershot wheel have been found (undershot wheels were typically Spanish; the overshot wheel was imported from the East Coast by Americans). Old records indicate houses, barns, and a stable on the property, as well as the mill, which continued in operation until the late nineteenth century.

Santa Fe, New Mexico

7

8

9

Santa Fe, New Mexico

10

Santa Fe, New Mexico

The William Griffiths bought the property in the late 1960s and commissioned architect William Lumpkins to design and supervise the modernization, enlargement, and general restoration. The Griffiths and Lumpkins agreed that nothing must be changed unless it was absolutely essential. The original rooms pictured here (7), as well as the grain rooms (up the stairway), were kept intact. The undulating floor in the small room that is thought to be stable boy's quarters (9), and the marvelous rough-hewn, worn, and mellowed old doors give visible testimony to centuries of use. Finest of all are the early windows, with closely spaced mullions that originally held sheets of mica to let in the light, before glass was available for window panes.

The group of buildings shown here (10, 11) are joined by common walls and occasionally interrupted by small inner courtyards. They were built as housing for servants, on De Vargas Street (the oldest street in America) in the Barrio de Analco. *Analco* means "other side of the water," which describes its location in relation to the center of Santa Fe. Thick walls and Indian pottery found at the site indicate early construction, but later additions were probably built about 1890–1900. At one time this group of houses was a red-light district, and by the mid-1960s, its dwellings had become filthy little one- or two-room hovels. However, when urban renewal, planning to demolish the entire complex, tore down one of the end buildings whose thick walls indicated early eighteenth-century construction, citizens were aroused.

Architect William Lumpkins enlisted a group of Santa Fe citizens who raised $250,000 to purchase the buildings. A computer company eventually bought them after Lumpkins persuaded them that the buildings could be adapted for a training center without changing their basic structure. Lumpkins designed the conversion. As in the Griffith house, he has saved everything that could be saved, and faithfully restored the rest, working with plasterers to teach them how to retain the bumps and bulges in early walls as they repaired them.

12

"Let no evil pass thy threshold" is the meaning of the hex signs over the doorway (*12*). Found under layers of white paint, they were returned to their original rust color by the present owners as they lovingly restored this 1710 saltbox house in Guilford (*color, page 18*).

The house was built by a grandson of Governor Leete on the land originally granted to the family, and descendants who lived here helped defend the area when the British crossed Long Island Sound to attack the community in the revolutionary war. In the eighteenth century the corner cupboard in the front room served as a post office; mail for the neighborhood was dropped off there and outgoing letters left on its shelves for collection (*13*).

Lived in by many generations of Leetes, the house had become a derelict by the 1930s. It was rescued by an antique dealer who persuaded members of the family, still living in Guilford, to sell it to her. She partially restored the house as a home and antique shop, and sold it, in 1959, to the present owners.

They have worked as carefully and patiently as archeologists to learn the house's secrets, enjoying every discovery. "You must take your time and let the house talk to you—never be in a hurry. Keep an open mind, without preconceived notions. Study other houses of the period in the vicinity; if your house doesn't speak loud and clear, maybe another house will. If you are trying to match original paint colors, look for a place that was not exposed to sunlight—inside a door jamb, for instance." Sound advice, from people who have accomplished a flawlessly beautiful restoration.

Though most of the house is unpainted, as it would have been when it was built, an upstairs bedroom is decorated in the eighteenth-century manner with buttermilk paint. Buttermilk or sour milk was used with dry pigment—in this case, iron oxide, which produces a deep red. It takes several days for the smell to go away, but this particular paint job is in its tenth year.

To repair the walls, the owners bought vermiculite plaster, and did the plastering themselves, rather than hiring professionals, so the result would not be smooth. Holes above mantels left by stovepipes used in a later period have been filled with coffee cans and plastered over. The coffee cans have been made into time capsules, containing letters, toys, and coins for future restorers.

Portsmouth, New Hampshire

Many eighteenth-century clapboard houses on the narrow streets of Portsmouth would probably still be wretched slums had it not been for the successful rescue of Strawberry Banke. The story is an important one, for it was the first time (in 1957) that citizens rose up and refused to allow historic houses to be flattened by urban renewal. The ten-acre waterfront site was buried under urban blight, sick with the symptoms urban renewal had been designed to cure with the bulldozer. Its seventeenth- and eighteenth-century clapboard houses had become a miserable, dilapidated shanty town surrounded by junk yards full of the rusting remains of automobiles. The city government applied for urban renewal funds to wipe out this eyesore, but librarian Dorothy Vaughn knew what lay hidden there: the homes of sea captains, sailors, joiners, shipwrights, the blacksmith's forge, rope walk, mast yard, and a tavern visited by Washington, Lafayette, John Paul Jones, and Paul Revere. She alerted a group of citizens, who backed their objections with action. A special act of the New Hampshire legislature was required to allow urban renewal to restore rather than demolish, so members of the group went to Concord and lobbied for new legislation, which was passed just as demolition was about to begin.

Because of the efforts of a group of citizens, urban renewal was used to clean up the area, removing junk yards and demolishing inappropriate later structures. The city appropriated money to buy buildings, the state gave the Governor Goodwin house, which, along with several others, was moved to cleared sites in the restoration area. Townspeople gave contributions, endowments, and furnishings to restore several important houses as museums, and, by 1963, Strawberry Banke was open to the public. Its picturesque name was what Portsmouth was called in 1630 by its first settlers, who found wild strawberries growing on the river bank.

Strawberry Banke is still only half completed, but it has attracted many visitors. It has also encouraged people who love old houses to buy and restore homes on the adjacent blocks, which were in a similar state of dilapidation.

Near Strawberry Banke, the house shown on pages 34 and 35 was built in 1786 by ship owner Captain Charles Grace. Its mantels and decorative trim had long since vanished in a Greek revival updating in 1840. When the neighborhood deteriorated, it became a home for two families, but had already been bought and cleaned up before the present owner purchased it for restoration. She is an antique collector, and her son, a very talented joiner, who works with tools used in the eighteenth century, did most of the fine woodwork restoration in Strawberry Banke. He did all the work in this house, remaking moldings, mantels, and front door with hand wrought reproductions of the woodwork in similar local houses of the period.

Portsmouth, New Hampshire

A fine example of authentic restoration is the 1732 house whose bedroom is shown on page 36. The floor is painted as it was originally, and the wall color was matched with a small original patch left exposed in a corner behind a dresser. The marbleized woodwork of the mantel and moldings was uncovered and restored (both here and on the stairway) by an eighty-two-year-old German, trained in Berlin. The owners, both artists, are working slowly and carefully on the other rooms. On the living-room walls, they have uncovered two pieces of early wallpaper, and several painted stencils: a flower, a ship, and a parrot.

The house had a varied career and many owners, none of whom had the money to restore it or ruin it. It served as a church in the 1950s, as a brothel in the 1960s, and finally as a three-family house, with the rear yard full of junked automobiles.

Long before completing their own house, its owners became involved in restoration of four others, with partners—one the rescue of an important old store-residence on the verge of collapse. Most Portsmouth newcomers are also involved in multiple restorations. They consider the old buildings in Portsmouth's South End a great investment, and they like living in an old waterfront community with a totally mixed population.

Rebuilding this unusually steep, curved stairway (15) was one of the many challenges facing Burt Trafton when he bought an 1815 brick house in 1968. The balustrade had simply been ripped out and discarded when the previous owner wanted to move a wardrobe upstairs. Luckily there was enough left above to be copied, and Trafton was fortunate to have the work done by the skillful joiner who has since done most of the fine carpentry at Strawberry Banke. Though the building was in wretched shape, Trafton wanted a town house, and this one was so near Strawberry Banke as to be almost part of it. It provided an opportunity to exercise his lifelong restoration expertise, and made a suitable showcase for his fine collection of antiques. Trafton has restored three houses in Portsmouth (as well as two in South Berwick, Maine), and is a restoration consultant who has persuaded many other people to buy old houses.

16

Charleston, South Carolina

Though the United States had to wait until 1976 to celebrate its two-hundredth birthday, Charleston commemorated its three-hundredth anniversary in 1970. Unique among American cities, Charleston is a visual delight, a showcase of an architectural heritage that is preserved and treasured. Oddly enough, the city has a more Southern atmosphere than Savannah, Georgia, one hundred miles farther south. While Savannah has a wide variety of architectural styles imported from other regions, Charleston's appearance is homogeneous. A single style of domestic architecture, influenced by the West Indies and the climate, is repeated over and over—build-

ings one or two rooms wide, placed endwise to the street, on an angle to catch the breeze off the water, with columned porches, called piazzas, running along the full length of one side. Shown here (20) is the handsome doorway of such a house, which is being lovingly restored by a young doctor and his wife. The rotting balustrades of the piazzas have been replaced (21) and the entire exterior repainted a sparkling white, while the meticulous stripping of interior woodwork continues.

Poverty saved Charleston's architecture from modification by changing tastes or demolition. The Civil War left Charleston destitute; one vis-

itor described it as a city of "vacant houses, of widowed women, of rotted wharves, of deserted warehouses, of weed-wild gardens, of grass-grown streets, of acres of pitiful and voiceless barrenness." By the time Charleston's economy recovered, its citizens could take pride in the purity of an architectural heritage unsullied by mansard roofs and other Victorian additions.

Charleston, which has more genuine historic architecture than Williamsburg ever had before its reconstruction, was discovered by tourists after World War I. Having survived fires, earthquakes, and hurricanes, the city's buildings were then endangered by indiscriminate collectors, who carried off everything from ironwork and paneling to entire houses. This invasion forced Charleston to rediscover and protect itself.

The country's first historic district legislation was passed in Charleston in 1931, and the Historic Charleston Foundation was established in 1947. The Foundation has worked hard and tirelessly for preservation, restoration, and adaptive use, saving many individual buildings as

well as entire areas, pressing for underground installation of unsightly utility wires, and persuading the College of Charleston to restore and re-use countless buildings that would have been demolished during the school's expansion.

An outsider, hearing of Charleston's successes, as well as its physical beauty, might conclude that all its restoration work was done; this is not so. In 1973, Charlestonians raised $1 million to prevent an Atlanta developer from razing a dozen offices and warehouses to build an eight-story condominium. Though most of the Ansonborough area has been restored, one can still find shockingly derelict houses (16) standing cheek-by-jowl with their impeccably restored counterparts. More work remains to be done in the Wraggsborough, Harleston Village, and Radcliffeborough areas.

Ansonborough is a section of Charleston named after Captain George Anson, who is said to have won the land in a card game in 1726. The Historic Charleston Foundation began the rehabilitation of its many fine buildings (17) in

1959, with the purchase of seven houses (the Foundation inaugurated the use of the widely initiated revolving fund to save endangered houses). Two were completely restored by the Foundation to stimulate interest; then all were resold, with protective covenants, to individuals. However, long before this, in 1941, the Benjamin Kittredges had bought the 1712 William Rhett house and five other properties in Ansonborough.

The William Rhett house, whose dining room is shown here (22), is the oldest house still standing in Charleston. It was built on Rhett's plantation lands, which were of such size that the entire area was then called Rhettsbury. Colonel Rhett was vice-admiral of the province, and distinguished himself by repelling a French-Spanish naval attack on the city, and capturing the notorious pirate, Stede Bonnet, who was publicly hanged. The house survived a disastrous fire in 1838 because a creek that ran across the property stopped the flames that swept through the surrounding buildings.

The Benjamin Kittredges had spent three

winters renting in Charleston when they decided to look for a house to restore. They claim to have been unaware of the house's distinguished history when they first saw it, but decided to buy it even though their friends were "very angry with them" for moving into the middle of Ansonborough, which was an abysmal slum. The Rhett house was being used as a bordello: the madam occupied the dirt-floored cellar, and the living room and large room above were divided into cubicles where the prostitutes practiced their trade. There was only one bathroom, erected on stilts and tacked onto the outside of the building. The Kittredges saw only one room before they bought the house; the dining room with its unusual stucco decoration. The restoration they began, continued while they were in Washington where Mr. Kittredge served in the Navy, following Pearl Harbor. But they returned to Charleston in 1947, and enjoyed living in the house for the next twenty years. When Mrs. Kittredge's health required that she forsake Charleston for Arizona, she and her hus-band sold the house to friends, Mr. and Mrs. Bushrod B. Howard.

In addition to the restoration of private homes, much has been accomplished in downtown Charleston. Perhaps no other American city can claim a business center as handsome, historic, and architecturally important as Charleston's Broad Street, whose buildings exhibit a variety of architectural styles spanning three centuries (18, 19). The Exchange Building, for instance, was built in 1771. It was the meeting place of the Provincial Congress, which set up the first independent government established in America. American prisoners were held in its cellar when the British occupied Charleston. Another structure, of 1798, probably the oldest banking building in the United States, is still being used as a bank. The City Hall, built in 1801 as a bank, may be the earliest example of adaptive use in Charleston. There are also several early homes that are now being used as business offices, as well as fine examples of Victorian commercial buildings.

The Broad Street Beautification Committee was established within the Historic Charleston Foundation for the improvement and further protection of this important street. A master plan was drawn up showing a sketch of each building, with recommended colors. Painting and refurbishing, as well as removal of unsightly signs was carried out on a volunteer basis, but within two years all such signs were down and twenty buildings were painted. Ugly overhead utility wires were buried, and the city agreed to plant trees on both sides of the street. The Historic Charleston Foundation completed the program with plaques for each building, designating builders and dates of construction.

Though few cities have buildings as historic or distinguished as Charleston's, this is a concrete illustration proving that business districts do not have to be eyesores. A similar approach to façade restoration on nineteenth-century commercial structures has brought fine results in Marshall, Michigan, and Portland, Maine.

20

21

22

Newport, Rhode Island

23

Newport has long been associated with the opulent mansions of the wealthy. These splendid castles (referred to as cottages by their owners) still stud the rocky coast, but today they are almost obsolete—impractical to run without an army of servants. Long forgotten and fallen into ruin, the compact clapboard homes built by early settlers on streets near the port where the town began, are now being rediscovered and restored as homes (24, 26; color, page 48). Four hundred were built before 1830; 250 are pre-revolutionary. Newport was a very early settlement, founded in 1639 by refugees from religious intolerance. Its port prospered from trade in molasses, rum, sperm oil, and slaves until it was occupied by the British for two years during the Revolution. Then it suffered a decline; hence the absence of Federal-style buildings, which abound in neighboring Providence.

Restoration of early Newport houses began in 1963, when an Englishwoman, Mrs. Charles Pepys, formed an organization called Operation Clapboard. She bought up options and contracts to buy $60,000 worth of real estate (at the rate of $2,000–7,000 per house) on the assumption that she could find buyers before she had to take title to the property. She succeeded in placing thirty houses in the hands of people who would restore them. Ten years later, similar houses were selling for $20,000–25,000.

Operation Clapboard, joined by Oldport Association, continues to work toward the restoration of Newport; the latter functioning mainly as an educational organization. However, the Doris Duke Foundation has superceded Operation Clapboard in purchase and restoration activity, buying up all available houses to be restored and retained by the Foundation for rental.

Though there are still some houses in very bad shape indeed, the many strikingly handsome restorations would seem to indicate that Newport has won the battle for preservation. But this is not so; the inevitable supremacy of the automobile is taking its toll. The government is running a highway right through the center of town, cutting it off from the sea. Newport was built around the sea; it was the town's reason for existence. Many houses have been lost already, and more have been moved to new sites to avoid demolition. The moving of houses in Newport is a surprisingly old, and frequently used, custom.

The 1750 John Goddard house (25) was moved from the waterfront in 1868. It was built as the home of the renowned cabinetmaker, who lived there with his family of nine children. His workshop, built onto the rear of the house, was left behind when the house was moved. The house had stood vacant for six years before it was bought by Mr. and Mrs. Albert Henry in 1968. Prior to that, it had been used as a rooming house. The Henrys fell in love with it in spite of broken windows and holes in the roof. Mr. Henry, a school administrator, and his wife, a

Providence, Rhode Island

Newport, Rhode Island

24

25

teacher, have been ardent American antique collectors for thirty years. A 1965 article in *Antiques* magazine about the numerous inexpensive houses available for restoration in Newport, brought them from Long Island to look for a retirement home. They wanted to buy the Goddard house the moment they saw it, but it was boarded up by owners who planned to restore it themselves. Every two weeks for three years the Henrys spent weekends in a motel and drove around searching for a house. "With their hearts in their eyes," they kept returning to the Goddard house, until at last it was put on the market and they were able to buy it.

They worked on it weekends, until retirement enabled them to move in. First they removed everything that was not original to the house. A porch and dormer windows came off

the exterior. Inside they uncovered the fireplaces that had been walled up with beaver board covered with wallpaper. The original floors were found under several layers of later flooring. Finding that there were fourteen layers of paint on the living-room fireplace woodwork, and only eleven coats on the mantel shelf, they determined that the shelf had been added around 1810, so they removed it to uncover Goddard's original strong, but simple, paneling and molding *(color, page 45).*

Removing everything that was not original to the house created thirty-six truckloads of debris. Then came roof repair, pointing up the chimney, replacing broken windows, and the contracting of major work, such as plumbing, heating, and wiring. The interior work has been a labor of love, done gradually by the Henrys

themselves, who feel strongly about not over restoring *(23, 27).*

The interior is painted with colors they found in the earliest layers of paint; brown, red, gold, and green. Floors have been repainted, as they were in early Newport houses, with the same color that was found on the original boards. Furniture is arranged as it was in eighteenth-century pictures.

The blue exterior was one of the first in Newport. They arrived at the color by painting sample squares of plywood in many colors in the yard of their Long Island home, causing some perplexity among their neighbors. Their final choice was questioned by some Newporters, until the Henrys cited an advertisement in the eighteenth-century *Newport Mercury* for "a house of blue."

Newport, Rhode Island

Old Salem, North Carolina

Old Salem was carefully and methodically built by Moravians (a Germanic religious sect) as a planned community, with every detail set down on paper before a single brick was laid. Its restoration is in the same spirit, an almost too-perfect example of an ideal town, with every blade of grass in place. However, it is a living, working restoration, not just a museum—and who among us in the polluted, commercial twentieth century, would quarrel with perfection?

Salem—meaning peace—was founded in 1766 by devout, hard-working people, whose economic, as well as spiritual, lives were directed by the church. In 1913, Salem merged with the neighboring commercial and industrial town of Winston, to become Winston-Salem. Salem was gradually engulfed and nearly annihilated, as many of its sturdy, simple houses were destroyed, and others buried under ugly siding, hemmed in and smothered by commercial growth, covered with neon signs, and festooned with telephone wires and power cables.

28

29

In 1947, when a grocery store threatened to build a supermarket in the midst of Old Salem, the citizens were aroused. A zoning ordinance was passed in 1948 to protect the district from further encroachment, and in 1950, the non-profit corporation, Old Salem, Inc., was established. Private individuals, with assistance from local corporations and foundations, and city, county, and state governments, began acquiring property.

Nearly one hundred nonconforming structures were demolished, and some forty-eight buildings have been restored or reconstructed to date, as Old Salem approaches two-thirds completion of its restoration goals. Utility wires have been buried, street signs and lamp posts redesigned, through traffic diverted to a four-lane by-pass, and open spaces landscaped with trees, shrubs, grass, and flowers.

A number of exhibition buildings are open to the public as Old Salem makes an all-out bid for tourists; other buildings have been adapted as shops and professional offices.

But people also live here. Though there are strict rules governing outward appearances, and no building may be used for other than its original purpose, owners and renters may do as they please with interiors. However, those who choose to live here seem to be completely under the influence of their surroundings.

Residents are hard to find on Saturdays; they are all likely to be off antiquing at weekly auctions. George Waynick is such an incurable collector that his wife complains (with a twinkle of pride in her eyes) that as soon as she stores some of the overflow in the attic, he notices, and demands she put it back. Waynick's parents bought their house (31) in 1947, before Old Salem, Inc., was organized, when the neighborhood was a slum, and the house, divided into apartments, was in bad shape. It was built in 1830 by a German doctor, who had his office in the house and made medicines in the cellar.

Waynick's brother-in-law, George Wright, who rents the Lick-Boner house, makes handsome, aged-black tin chandeliers (as a hobby) that hang in his own house, as well as others in Old Salem. Many are copies of originals collected by Waynick; the one shown here was designed to cast a butterfly shadow on the wall (28). The Lick-Boner house on Salt Street was the first house restored by Old Salem, Inc. The clapboard (29) that had been added to the log structure in 1811 was stripped off to return it to the way it looked when carpenter Martin Lick built it as his home in 1787 (30). Writer John Henry Boner, who was born in the house, revisited it in later years and found it in such a sad state that he wrote a poem about it called "Broken and Desolate." He would be pleased if he could see it today, beautifully restored and filled with George Wright's fine antiques (32), handmade chandeliers, and painted canvas floor covering (color, page 57).

Among the restored buildings in Old Salem are the typically Moravian half-timbered houses. The one shown (33) was restored by Old Salem, Inc., and rented to a family.

33

Old Salem, North Carolina

Alexandria, Virginia

Alexandria's Old Town is a serene village on the doorstep of the nation's capital with concentrated blocks of charming houses; it is a living picture book of fine architecture, redolent with important historical associations. Young George Washington assisted the surveyor who laid out the city, owned a town house, helped found the first bank, school, and fire company. Robert E. Lee spent his boyhood in an Alexandria house, and the first blood of the Civil War was shed here. A statue of a soldier facing south in the middle of Washington Street marks the place where Alexandria's young men assembled before marching off to join the Confederacy, leaving a town torn apart in its proximity to the seat of government, with its heart in the South.

Alexandria's prosperity as a port began to decline with the rise of the railroads after the Civil War. By the turn of the century most of its old families had fled, and this wealthy, beautiful, historic town deteriorated for more than forty years, until it was a slum. The housing shortage of World War II was Alexandria's salvation, as home seekers from Washington discovered the brick houses across the Potomac. One of the first pioneers bought a distinguished town house in the block known as Gentry Row. She hesitated to invite her mother to see it until she had worked enough to restore it to fairly good condition. Her mother said not a word while regarding the neighborhood and looking over the house. Finally she turned to her daughter and said, "Don't you try to sell this house. Just give it to anybody who will take it off your hands, and get out of here."

Needless to say, that house is now an extremely valuable property. The lady, who did not take her mother's advice, was soon joined by others, as fine houses began emerging from cocoons of neglect, grime, and decay. Alexandria became a showplace once again, with street after street of handsome restored homes and many fine examples of adaptive use as well. The 1807 Bank of Alexandria and the historic 1752 Carlyle house, for many years completely neglected, are at last being restored. Open to the public by private owners, Carlyle house had dingy furniture, peeling paint, and no electricity; visitors were handed flashlights as they entered!

One would think that the battle was won in Alexandria, that the value of its architecture and history had been proven beyond dispute. Unfortunately, this is not so. Alexandria represents a microcosm of American restoration in its struggle to survive in the twentieth century. Restoration versus demolition has been a constant seesaw battle. The fact that the struggle is still not over may be symbolized by the recent destruction of an 1854 brick house for a motel site, countered by restoration of the lovely Greek revival Lyceum on Washington Street as a community cultural center.

34

35

36

Alexandria, Virginia

One of Alexandria's greatest problems is that it lies between the center of employment in Washington and the suburban homes of Fairfax County, and many people would prefer to replace Old Town with a superhighway. Urban renewal demolished many fine old houses on King Street (though a developer was ready to restore them) to make an ugly commercial street that is not even successful. According to local preservationists, the Chamber of Commerce is their enemy, and the business community has fought against restoration in favor of high-rise apartments.

The melodramatic rescue of the Lyceum typifies the turmoil behind Alexandria's serene façade. Knowing that demolition would begin the next morning, two hundred people sat watching, with tears running down their faces, while the city council voted not to appropriate funds to save the handsome community meeting hall where John Quincy Adams once spoke. The building was saved at the last minute when one man reconsidered and decided to change his vote. Its restoration is a proud, shining symbol—one more victory in a war that never seems to be won.

The row of small brick houses shown here (36) was built between 1804 and 1820 as housing for working men. Revival of smaller houses like these had to wait until the larger ones became less available and more costly. This block was still a shambles until the late 1960s. Jean Keith, an expert on Alexandria history who is extremely active in restoration battles, bought the center house in 1961. It had been a rooming house for itinerant contractors' workers, then a warehouse, condemned for human habitation. Keith found it full of debris, and with the rear half of the ground floor missing. He did ninety per cent of the manual labor himself, with a cooperative contractor who returned when needed. He replaced missing mantels with some of the same period that he salvaged from Baltimore houses that were being demolished. He stripped many layers of paint off the façade to reveal the natural, aged brick.

The exquisite house built about 1800 by a sea captain from Salem, Massachusetts, became the winter residence of Thomas, Lord Fairfax and his son, Dr. Orlando Fairfax, in 1815. When Dr. Fairfax went to Richmond to become surgeon-general of the Confederacy, the Union expropriated the house for its headquarters and a hospital. Later one of Fairfax's daughters married Gouverneur Morris of Philadelphia, who was able to buy it back.

The Winfield Scott Macgills bought the house in 1962, and Mrs. Macgill, an artist, worked for the next three years with painstaking care and skill on its restoration and furnishing. The incredibly beautiful fanlight of the arched front door is repeated by a twin arch and fanlight on a doorway at the end of the wide entrance hall (color, page 58).

A fine Georgian house (34, 35), set far back from the street, was built prior to 1752, when it was decreed that all subsequent buildings should be built on the front property line. People who purchased the original lots in 1749 had to agree to build within two years or forfeit the property, so the first owner of this lot built a "flounder" house facing Washington Street, in anticipation of a later building, of which the flounder would become a wing. (A flounder, common to Alexandria, is like a peak-roofed house sliced down the middle, frequently built as a wing, or ell.)

Between 1800 and 1810, the second owner, William Fowle, built the main house, with its lovely doorway facing Prince Street, perpendicular to the original flounder, which became a rear wing. Fowle had eighteen children, several of whom left their names clearly incised on window panes in five or six different places in the house.

A descendant of Fowle's, a woman in her nineties, had been living here for many years alone before Major General and Mrs. Walker bought it in 1969. The house had slowly deteriorated; the living room, whose floor had sunk four inches on one side due to rotting joists, was dark and dreary, and the shutters were falling off. As a career army family, the Walkers had roamed the world for thirty years. When General Walker learned he was doomed to die of a brain tumor, he determined to leave a home for his wife. He planned and supervised the restoration, with much of the work done by young soldiers moonlighting from the army base. General Walker died before the work was completed, but his legacy of love and courage won an award from the Alexandria Association for a restoration that "faithfully and well reflects the traditional architectural style of Alexandria."

Philadelphia, Pennsylvania

This brick house, built in 1759, and later owned by a major in Washington's army, was a vile-smelling flophouse *(39)* when it was bought by the C. Jared Ingersolls. They determined to restore it to its eighteenth-century condition, adding modern conveniences as unobtrusively as possible *(37; color, page 46)*. Under layers of old linoleum were the two-hundred-year-old random-width Pennsylvania pine floors, and to their "amazement and great joy," when they tore off the boards covering the fireplace openings, they found the iron firebacks, marble facings, and hearths. They painted every room in the house, except one, in the original color, determined by scraping back nineteen layers of old paint with a scalpel *(38)*.

The Ingersolls played an important role in the resurrection of Society Hill, and in reversing a well-established Philadelphia tradition against living in the city. Adjacent to Independence Hall, this site of William Penn's original American colony was a disaster area (called the Bloody Fifth Ward) until the city of Philadelphia acted to rescue it in 1959. Mayor Richardson Dilworth inaugurated a sweeping urban renewal plan, breaking precedent with past policies of total demolition, to save the largest concentration of eighteenth-century houses remaining anywhere in America. Houses were bought up and resold to individuals for restoration under strict historic controls.

Today a walk along the brick sidewalks of Society Hill (named for William Penn's Free Society of Traders) is a delightful experience, not to be missed by visitors to Philadelphia *(40)*. Its economic impact has been enormous, as 120 blocks have been converted from slum to well-to-do status, and its highly visible success has given impetus to the revival of other city areas.

37

39

38

Annapolis, Maryland

Annapolis, Maryland's capital since 1695, and America's capital at the end of the American Revolution, was the scene of the ratification of peace with England by the Continental Congress. This important historic city, site of some of America's finest Georgian architecture, was on the verge of oblivion when some of its citizens began to fight for its life in 1952.

The waterfront view had been cut off by eyesores, there were twenty vacant stores in the town center, and important buildings were falling victim to speculators who were razing them for parking lots and high-rise towers. Businessmen and residents fled. A mayoral candidate actually proposed that the state capital be moved to Baltimore, and Annapolis leveled and turned over to the Naval Academy.

Historic Annapolis, Inc., has reversed the blight, causing a 112-per-cent increase in property values and a boom in tourism. The view of the waterfront was regained by demolition of buildings that obstructed it. Countless significant buildings have been saved, among them the 1723 Shiplap house, now headquarters of Historic Annapolis (a small building that had housed twenty-seven people), and the old city market. The latter involved an interesting legal maneuver. In 1784, eight merchants had donated the space for the original market (the present market was built in 1858). Recently, a group of influential citizens wanted to use the site for parking space, so the city government voted to demolish it and threw out the tenants. However, Historic Annapolis's lawyer found that the deed stated that the property should revert to the original donors if it were not used as they had intended. Three descendants of the donors were found, and suit was filed on behalf of the heirs. While the suit was in court, a new mayor and city council were elected on a historic-preservation platform, and money was budgeted for restoration of the market. Another legal tactic frequently used by Historic Annapolis to rescue properties for restoration is environmental easement. This is similar to a protective covenant, and involves placing a permanent legal rider on a property deed, forbidding demolition or exterior alteration. The organization is currently involved in a campaign that is sorely needed by Annapolis and many other cities: removal of unsightly utility wires that mar the townscape.

Among the major achievements of Historic Annapolis is the restoration of the 1765 William Paca house and gardens (45). Paca was governor of Maryland, a signer of the Declaration of Independence, and credited by George Washington as a major contributor to the success of the Revolution. His mansion in the center of Annapolis, a splendid example of the distinctive five-section Maryland style of architecture, was threatened by plans for an office-apartment de-

42

43

44

velopment. The prospect of the destruction of the heart of their historic district mobilized preservationists to conceive an alternate plan, involving restoration of the Paca house and gardens. The plan, which will make the Paca house a self-supporting landmark through its use as an official U.S. State Department guest house for visiting international dignitaries, was accepted by the Maryland General Assembly, and funds for purchase were appropriated in 1965.

The mansion, though in desperate need of restoration, was still intact, but the gardens had been buried and forgotten for over a hundred years, hidden under a bus station, parking lot, and a two-hundred-room hotel that all but enveloped the Paca house. The gardens on the two-acre site were apparently among the finest in America. On the basis of documentary evidence in three eighteenth-century letters, and the background of the Charles Willson Peale painting of William Paca, archeological excavation and restoration has recreated the gardens as they were two hundred years ago. A surprising number of the original features were found: the base of a crumbling wall, fragments of limestone steps, foundations of three buildings, location of a Chinese Chippendale bridge that was known to have spanned a brook, five terraces, the outline of a natural lake, a lower-level wilderness garden, and an elaborate system of water conduits. Both the house and garden

restoration are being carried out with consummate care, resulting in an authentic, eighteenth-century gem for Annapolis and America.

Another of the fine private homes of Annapolis is the 1765 Ridout house whose rear exterior view is shown here (41). George Washington was a frequent guest here, and Martha once left her nightcap behind. This house, which has always been occupied by members of the family that built it, is more an example of preservation than restoration. The arch in the entrance hall (42) required minor restoration after a Victorian lamp was removed from the keystone. The clock, found in pieces in the attic, was reassembled, and its wheels rebuilt by master craftsman George Jones of Newcastle, Maine, who researched it in Boston and Philadelphia museums. The hardware and charming doorbell (43) are original to the house.

The small houses on Cornhill Street (44), built about 1800 as dwellings and shops for artisans, were the first to be restored as private homes, beginning in the late 1940s. Because Annapolis became a forgotten city after the Revolution, when new, bigger ships could no longer use its harbor, residents were too poor to maintain these houses, or destroy them by modernization and alteration. It is said that "once you couldn't sell a house on Cornhill Street, and now you can't buy one," as property values have doubled and tripled since restoration began.

Annapolis, Maryland

Providence, Rhode Island

The restoration of Providence's Benefit Street into a charming Mile of History lined with colorful, revolutionary clapboard houses, came about through the combined efforts of community organization and the heroic action taken by one woman. High on the rim of College Hill overlooking the marble dome of the state capitol, the early homes of merchants and craftsmen were built when Roger Williams settled the town. They were in a sorry state, surrounded by debris, and rendered unrecognizable by dilapidation, cobbled-on porches, and asbestos siding. Several blocks were slated for demolition by Brown University in a plan for expansion. Aroused citizens formed the Providence Preservation Society, and with funding from a government grant, did an impressive study evaluating the Benefit Street houses and formulating a proposal for their restoration combined with urban renewal of streets, traffic, and other neighborhood facilities.

However impressive this landmark study, nothing was happening in the way of physical change on Benefit Street until Mrs. Malcolm G.

47

46

Chace, Jr., quietly went to work on her own. She bought up some thirty houses and employed a contractor to strip away all later additions, rip out obsolete plumbing and wiring, then weatherproof and paint the exteriors. Once the beautifully simple forms were revealed, their obvious potential made resale for restoration possible. Mrs. Chace eventually recouped her investment and performed an invaluable service to the community and the American architectural heritage.

The first families that bought houses were faced with the problem of all urban pioneers: having to live in the midst of poverty and slum conditions. None of them regret it. In fact, Linda Miller, an early homeowner on Benefit Street, says it changed the direction of her life, as she became involved in school-administration work with the black community.

Mrs. Miller was looking for a country home for her large family when she fell in love with the 1780 James Burr house on Benefit Street—which she decided to buy in one day *(46; color, page 47)*. Its deceptively small façade conceals a seventeen-room interior, as it extends back and downhill to two gardens in the rear.

Though the house had been gutted by Mrs. Chace, Mrs. Miller bought it without really seeing the downstairs rear because the floors were caving in. It had served as a rooming house for three or four families, and the backyard was a mass of rubble.

Linda Miller heartily agrees with the admonition of so many others who have restored old houses—to work very slowly and let the house "speak to you." But she learned the hard way, by doing it all wrong. She readily admits wasting thousands of dollars remedying errors. She began by moving walls to change the room layout. Having hired an expensive New York City decorator, she came to the realization that nothing he proposed would work. She says that the house began screaming at her, "Please put me back." She fired the decorator and did exactly that, having come to the conclusion that the house had a character of its own that should not be violated. Today she says, "These houses

Providence, Rhode Island

were beautifully thought out. They knew what they were doing when they designed them."

She bitterly regrets removing the bellying of the exterior wall, and the loss of the beehive oven in the fireplace. The contractor persuaded her that he could not make the chimney work properly without removing the oven. She wishes that the experts at the Providence Preservation Society had "tied her to a chair" and refused to set her free until she agreed to save the oven, which is now irretrievably lost.

The story of the antique cupboard standing between two windows in the front room is an intriguing tale of coincidence, or fate (49). On a trip to Maine six or seven years after she bought the house, Mrs. Miller had resolved to stay out of antique shops, but she saw one she was unable to resist. Though she is not normally attracted to primitive pieces, she was impelled to open the door of one old cupboard. Inside the door was attached a typed inscription stating that the cupboard was made by order of James Burr on the occasion of receiving a new set of china, in 1807. She was able to verify through Burr's will that a cupboard with seventy-seven pieces of china stood in the very room where she placed the piece she found in Maine. The cupboard was made for Burr by Deacon James Daggett of Rehoboth. Mrs. Miller had bought mantels from Daggett's house to replace those that were missing from the Burr house.

The Daniel Pearce house (47) was built in 1781 in the conventional central-chimney style, similar to the James Burr house. About 1850 it was converted to a Lightning Splitter, the current theory being that this unique shape would prevent lightning from striking the house.

The William Ashton, Jr., house may have been built as early as 1759, but the lower floor was reconstructed in 1789 after it was damaged in a fire. The elaborate façade details and the exceptionally fine woodwork in the front parlor were added during this later rebuilding (48, 50). In stripping off layers of old paint, owner Donald Nelson found that delicate curves and other details of the mantel decoration were made of pewter.

Natchez, Mississippi

Most of the extraordinarily beautiful houses of Natchez had fallen into a tragic state of ruin by the early years of the twentieth century. Natchez women, born and bred to a tradition of Southern hospitality, never faltered in their love and appreciation of fine homes and the antique furnishings that complement their handsome interiors. But for eighty years there was simply no money to maintain them. Roofs leaked and plaster cornices fell from the walls.

They were built when a preponderance of American wealth was concentrated in this small settlement on a bluff over the Mississippi River; Natchez boasted more millionaires than anywhere in the United States except New York City. Fortunes were made from cotton grown across the river in Louisiana and shipped out on steamboats. The Civil War spelled an end to Southern prosperity. Homes were saved from destruction only because Natchez women swallowed their pride and entertained their enemy invaders. After the war, with steamboats replaced by railroads, and labor to farm the cotton fields gone with the abolition of slavery, the town was left with no source of income.

But, in 1932, an audacious scheme by Natchez women saved the houses once more. It began when they were asked by the state to organize a garden-club tour. Gardens were in such a sorry state that Mrs. J. Balfour Miller conceived the idea of opening their houses instead. It was in the midst of the depression, and banks were closed. People said they were crazy, and their husbands laughed at them. But Mrs. Miller, who saw an opportunity to restore their deteriorating homes, began traveling around the country to stir up interest. With a handful of mediocre slides to show on church lanterns, she went wherever she could beg a ride, to talk to any group willing to listen. The ladies put on hoop skirts and opened their homes for the first Natchez Pilgrimage. People came. And the admission fees began paying for sorely needed repairs, restoration, and maintenance.

The Pilgrimage became an annual spring event, which has kept the Natchez women hard at work, not only restoring their own homes, but saving others as well. Soon after launching the Pilgrimage, they restored Connelly's Tavern (ca. 1795) where the first American flag was raised over Natchez. They also rescued Longwood, an extravagant octagonal mansion that was left half-completed when workmen dropped their tools to fight in the Civil War, and never came back.

Perhaps their most ambitious undertaking was Stanton Hall. One of Natchez's most magnificent mansions, it was threatened with demolition and the sale of its interiors—its ornate woodwork, marble mantels, and silver hardware. No one could afford to restore it or live in it. Two members of the Pilgrimage Garden Club signed a note, and Stanton Hall was beautifully restored and furnished as a museum and club headquarters. It also serves as an elegant setting for parties, as well as accommodation for invited guests. The most recent Garden Club restoration was King's Tavern, one of the earliest buildings in Natchez, built before 1789.

Within the last ten years fine houses have still been lost for replacement by filling stations, and some remain on the critical list. Others were on the brink of ruin before they were restored. Mistletoe, a charming house dating from 1807, had its walls papered with newspaper, its cypress-paneled sitting room painted with white enamel. Chickens were housed in Brandon Hall (54) before a Texas family bought it and began repairing its beautiful plaster cornices and medallions, rebuilding its rotted porch, and replacing broken columns. Union troops once rode cavalry horses through the entrance hall (51) and drawing room of Monteigne, built in 1855, and smashed the crystal chandeliers because the owner was a Confederate major general. Others, among the numerous great houses that have been restored, are Cherokee (52) and Edgewood (53).

Some of the most severe deterioration in Natchez took place downtown in the old Spanish section where Dr. and Mrs. George Moss have been working since 1964 on Texada (56, 57). Many people have the mistaken idea that all Natchez houses were built in the mid-nineteenth century just prior to the Civil War. The fact is that many of them date back to the late eighteenth century. This one is thought to have been built in 1792, just after the property was first mentioned in a Spanish land grant. Though America took possession of Natchez in 1797, Spanish settlers stayed on, and in 1798, this property was sold at auction to Don Manuel Garcia de Texada (Te-hada). In 1806, described in the *Natchez Gazette* as a "large, elegant and commodious new brick house," it became a hotel and tavern. In 1817, it was purchased for $10,000 by Judge Edward Turner, Esq., who later divided it in half and gave it to his two daughters. However, by the time Dr. and Mrs. Moss

bought it, it had been divided into ten apartments with eight kitchens and six baths. Though everyone was sure the building was beyond rehabilitation (55) and would have to be torn down, the Mosses, who "liked the style and feeling of it," accepted the challenge of restoration.

First they renovated the kitchen and servant's quarters in a separate building in the rear and moved in, so that they could take their time with the main house. So many changes had been made since the house was built that they spent two and a half years working with an architect to decide on the best way to restore it. During this time they were able to collect old doors, mantels, and other materials from nearby sites as replacements for missing pieces.

Considerable work had to be done on the exterior. The second front door had to be eliminated, and the Mosses wanted to remove the stucco that had been added seventy-five to a hundred years ago. There was some doubt that the old brick could be exposed because of damage from scoring when the stucco was applied. But two local bricklayers took on the job as a personal responsibility, removing damaged bricks and reversing them, and sanding the rest by hand. Decorative trim was found hidden under gutters, and wood shingles were concealed under layers of roofing. Rotted and missing trim was copied, and shingles were replaced with cedar shakes. The one intact, original dormer was reproduced to make a second. A substitute for the missing front door was found on a house in the vicinity that was being demolished.

Inside, the procedure was repeated. Much was broken, missing, or destroyed, but enough pieces were found throughout the house to provide models for reproduction. The house may have been built by East Coast artisans, which would explain its resemblance to New England architecture. It features solid brick interior walls with heart cypress (termite-proof) floors laid directly over the ground on sills, which are not tied into the walls—the workmen described them as "laid agin it."

Though construction began in 1970, the Mosses have just finished half the house—the first floor and part of the second (color, page 75). But their restoration has made a significant difference to the rejuvenation of the downtown area, and everyone is extremely grateful.

52

Natchez, Mississippi

53

54

55

56

Mobile, Alabama

58

For many years, known as Yesterhouse, this building (59) was associated with stories of treasure, secret rooms, ghosts, and outlaws. There were turn-of-the-century tales of an apparition of a young woman said to have been hanged there during construction of the house, and another ghost of a man killed by lightning on the grounds. Under the fountain in the rear garden, there is an underground chamber with only one entrance, capped by a stone slab. Rumors and speculation associate this subterranean room and supposed connecting tunnels with pirates or outlaw gangs. Small wonder that it was known as a ghost house, as it stood surrounded with overgrown thickets and vines, its roof leaking and its paint peeling. The entire interior was a gloomy gray, with cotton shag wall-to-wall carpeting nailed to the floors. The last owners, who had inherited the house, never really wanted to live in it, and when their marriage ended, they moved out, leaving a son to camp out in one room while the unloved house deteriorated.

It was built in 1840, in Spring Hill, then a country summer retreat for city dwellers, and named Carolina Hall, for the native state of Charlestonian William Alfred Dawson, a cotton factor, who constructed it as his home. Dawson made his fortune buying cotton from Alabama planters, and shipping the bales from the port of Mobile to Atlantic Coast and English manufacturing markets. He brought back many purchases from Britain to adorn his magnificent house, as well as a bride from Edinburgh.

When it went on the market, standing on more than seven acres of valuable suburban real estate, it appeared that no one would be able to afford the price of purchase and restoration. Since it was outside the limits of Mobile's historic districts, there was little that could be done by the Mobile Historic Development Commission to save the house. At last the situation was happily resolved when a real-estate saleswoman arranged to divide the tract so that the house could be sold separately on one acre, while the remaining land went for building sites.

In 1972, after arrangements were made to break up the estate, the house was bought by Dr. and Mrs. Louie C. Wilson as a home for their young family. They have restored it, brightened the splendidly proportioned rooms with fresh colors, and highlighted with white the extraordinarily beautiful architectural details (60, 61; color, page 76).

Many of Mobile's historic houses have been preserved and protected through the efforts of the Mobile Historic Development Commission. Two historic districts, DeTonti Square and Church Street East, were created in 1962, and a third, Oakleigh Garden, was added in 1969. The Commission has fought long and hard to save Mobile's endangered buildings, achieving some notable triumphs, as well as suffering some tragic defeats. Most prevalent, and characteristic of the city's architecture, is the classic brick town house, with long front windows to the floor, framed by lacy ironwork galleries. Many of these handsome houses have been recycled in the DeTonti Square area, most as professional offices, and in one case, twin houses joined as a hotel.

One of the Commission's outstanding accomplishments was rescue of the 1859 Hamilton house (58) in the Church Street district. An urban renewal plan called for razing the entire block for construction of an auditorium. Thanks to efforts by the Commission, a compromise was reached, and the auditorium was moved back about a hundred feet. One house was sacrificed to make way for a landscaped plaza connecting the auditorium to the park on Church Street, but the remaining houses were saved. The Hamilton house, which had been divided up into seven apartments, was beautifully restored as a home by Mrs. Edwin K. Smith, who agreed to open it for occasional house tours.

The 1820s Bishop Portier house (62) is a fine example of a Creole cottage, an architectural style typical of Mobile and Louisiana. Portier, the first Catholic bishop of Mobile, made it his residence, and all subsequent bishops continued this custom until the last two. It had been standing vacant for a number of years, until a young lawyer and his wife, concerned about its plight, agreed to move their family in from the suburbs to live in it. Though the Catholic church still owns it, they have done considerable restoration work at their own expense.

Directly opposite stood the 1859 Durand house, demolished after the bishop had refused all pleas and proposals to save it. Initially, he planned to raze it in 1971, to build a thirteen-story apartment building for the elderly. However, when application for HUD funds was rejected because plans included demolition of an historic building, the high-rise was built on a site across the street. Refusing to sell the building at any price, or to consider any sort of compromise, he went ahead, and in November, 1974, (in the words of *Preservation News*) the Federal-style building became federal-style rubble.

60

62

Ste. Genevieve, Missouri

An eighteenth-century French town in Missouri? It sounds unlikely, but Ste. Genevieve, just south of St. Louis, was part of the Louisiana Territory and an important French outpost in the New World. Founded in 1723–35 as a port on the Mississippi River for shipping lead that was mined nearby, it was nearly wiped out by the river in 1785. Houses that were not destroyed by the flood were moved, and the town started over on higher ground a mile or two away.

The early Creole houses were built of vertical logs, either set directly in the ground (poteaux en terre) or on stone foundations (poteaux sur solle), the gaps between filled with bouzillage, a mixture of clay, mud, and animal hair, and covered with planks. Their distinctive pitched roofs, with deep overhang, provided galleries all around the houses. Under porches, the vertical log construction can still be seen, and in some of the attics, one can see the original, pegged Norman truss framework.

There are a number of these vertical log houses left in Ste. Genevieve, but only a few are visible, because many are concealed under artificial siding or otherwise distorted. Some half-dozen houses built in the late eighteenth century have been restored as museums and are open to the public. The best of these is the Amoreaux house, authentically restored and filled with a remarkable collection of American antiques by Mr. and Mrs. Norbert Donze. The Donzes also restored the Beauvais house, and converted Mr. Donze's boyhood home, a nineteenth-century brick house, into the Inn St. Gemme-Beauvais, combining modern comfort with antique charm.

Mr. and Mrs. Bernard Schram have contributed much loving labor to the restoration of their home, the historic Jean-Baptiste Valle house (62), which was probably built in 1787, and has been in Mrs. Schram's family since 1865. Though the interior was altered during its continuous occupation through the years, the exterior is typical of the Creole cottage style that is common to Ste. Genevieve, to Louisiana, and to Mobile, Alabama.

There are a number of people who have been working hard and earnestly to save and restore all of these unusual early houses through the Foundation for Restoration of Ste. Genevieve. Their aim seems to be the creation of an ideally restored community such as Old Salem. They already attract many tourists, who visit their houses and join in their Jour de Fête. However, they have never succeeded in passing legislation to protect endangered properties, and are hampered by lack of money. There is bitterness over the $30,000 spent by the government's Economic Development Administration in 1966 on a lavish master plan that is almost totally useless. An architectural team from St. Louis, ignorant of local history and problems, cavalierly drew up plans for parking lots and new buildings on the sites of historic houses and school property. Fortunately, there were no funds available to carry it out.

St. Louis, Missouri

Ever since he watched the demolition of a great old mansion when he was five years old, Timothy Conley wanted to own such a house. He found his house on Lafayette Park in a section of St. Louis considered dangerous, and slated to be demolished for an expressway.

There were condemnation notices on the dilapidated mansion, but when a prostitute leaning out of a window invited him inside, Conley accepted so that he could see the interior. It was in appalling condition. Though there were no longer any functioning utilities, sixty-two people lived there—eight in the drawing room alone. There were gaping holes in ceilings and floors, and the woodwork was enameled in a gaudy carnival of colors: the drawing-room mantel was purple, and the stairway spindles alternated purple, blue, orange, and brown. In spite of what he saw, Tim Conley bought the house three days later for $12,500.

Conley asked city officials to hold off on condemnation proceedings for six months. In those six months he removed eighty-three truckloads of debris, cleaned up, painted, and had new plumbing, heating, and wiring installed. One of the first things that he had done was the repair and painting of the exterior, stunning passers-by, who stopped and stared in disbelief. This highly visible change on desolate Lafayette Square, plus newspaper stories and other publicity, encouraged several other people to buy houses in the area within a few weeks. Eight months later, in the spring of 1970, more homes were bought for restoration, and by 1974, five years after Tim Conley bought the Blair-Huse mansion (64), two-thirds of the houses in the Lafayette Square area (some two hundred houses) were in the process of restoration. The Lafayette Square Restoration Committee regularly attracts ten thousand people to their house tours, netting $20,000. The crime rate has dropped by sixty per cent. Houses are bought within a day or so after being put on the market, and those that are in too bad condition to attract buyers are purchased, repaired and resold by the Lafayette Square Restoration Committee with the help of a revolving fund established with the aid of a loan from the National Trust for Historic Preservation. New stores and antique shops are flourishing, and an old police station has been restored as a visitors' center, as a steady stream of sightseers is attracted to the neighborhood every Sunday.

The path to this phenomenal success was not without thorns. There had been talk of an expressway to be built through the area as far back as the 1940s and 1950s. By 1971, the threat became real, with the road slated to go right through Lafayette Park. A passionate political battle was fought. The turning point came when a new administration sympathetic to preservation was elected, and at the same time, Lafayette Square was named an historic district listed on the National Register, which precludes use of federal funds to destroy it.

And so another great neighborhood of fine old homes is restored to useful life, if not quite its former splendor. This was an enclave of opulent country estates, where at least fifteen people of national importance built mansions. Conley's house was built by Montgomery Blair (of Blair House in Washington) in 1843. In the late 1860s, it was bought by millionaire William Huse, who employed St. Louis's most distinguished architect, George I. Barnett (designer of the governnor's mansion) to enlarge it, adding a drawing room and a new front entrance.

Tim Conley plans to restore it to its 1870s grandeur. He has been working for five years on restoration of the drawing-room ceiling (it was half gone, with floor joists showing through) recreating the missing decoration with latex molds, and applying gold leaf *(frontispiece)*. He has done all the plastering, floor repair, woodwork stripping, and even some of the plumbing himself, though he claims he never lifted a finger in his life before he bought the house on his twenty-first birthday.

Marshall, Michigan

Marshall was always a loser. In the 1840s, its citizens were so certain that their town would be chosen as the state capital that they built a governor's mansion. It was never to be occupied; they lost to Lansing by one vote. In 1847, when they refused to surrender a runaway slave who had lived in the town for several years, they were sued by the former owner and fined heavily for their good deed. In 1873, Marshall just missed becoming a major railroad terminal. And finally, its thriving patent medicine business of the 1890s was wiped out by federal legislation.

The town slept until well into the twentieth century. When it woke up, it found it had something very special. Something it never would have had if it had been a winner. Like legendary Brigadoon, it is an almost ideal, perfectly preserved little town. It is what American towns should look like, and don't. In the middle of Michigan, halfway between Lake Michigan and Lake Huron, and Chicago and Detroit, it is a peaceful oasis set among gently rolling hills. Its clean, wide streets bordered with huge old trees, meander among homes of all sizes, without commercial intrusion. There are no slums; even the poorer houses look neat and decently maintained.

The architectural variety is quite wonderful, with a somewhat whimsical, light-hearted quality. Greek revival homes come in all sizes, and there is Victorian gingerbread *(67),* Gothic revival with lacy bargeboards, Italianate villas topped with extraordinary pagoda-roofed cupolas or square towers *(68),* and the delightfully outlandish Hawaiian-Victorian Honolulu house *(69).*

Harold C. Brooks is credited with being the town's benefactor, responsible for awakening interest in preservation and restoration. He bought the fine 1840 Greek revival Fitch mansion *(66),* perched high on a hill at the edge of town, in 1921. A short time later, he also purchased the handsome stone Greek revival house across the street, because it was endangered. (These houses share an unusual feature found only in Marshall and Rochester, New York: an uneven number of columns on a Greek revival façade.) He eventually owned twelve houses, became mayor, and helped build the town hall, fire station, police station, and post office.

Marshall's renaissance was brought about by house tours. They began in 1964 as kitchen tours, organized to benefit the church, and evolved into annual house tours which were taken over by the Historical Society in 1967. To their surprise, Marshall's citizens began to realize that people would come from Chicago, Detroit, Indianapolis, and Toledo to see their homes. New interest and appreciation was awakened in old houses. In 1973, the tour drew ten thousand people, grossing $30,000. There is no difficulty in getting loans for purchase or

65

restoration, because even the bankers live in old houses. In fact, a new, recently opened bank offers checks printed with pictures of five Marshall houses.

Since the tours began, houses have doubled or tripled in value. Between 1960 and 1970, assessed valuation increased from $22 million to $40 million, bringing a fourteen per cent *decline* in the real-estate tax rate because of the increase in the tax base.

A real-estate broker, who handsomely adapted an old house as his office, has found his walk-in business tripled. The business district has also benefited from restoration. In 1967 there were fifteen to twenty empty stores on Main Street. The Chamber of Commerce, worried about this situation and fearful about a proposed shopping center, worked with the Historical Society on a plan to refurbish store façades. It was done on a private basis, with a sketch provided showing how the building might look after restoration. There are no longer empty stores, and customers are even

coming from out of town to shop.

Oakhill *(65, 70)* is one of twin houses built in 1858 by brothers-in-law. In 1948, it had been closed up for eighteen years, with much of the furniture left inside. Though enough heat was kept in the house to preserve the furnishings, there was restoration work to be done when it was bought by decorator Jacque Minick and her husband Harold, an industrial designer (who works in a converted mill over a waterfall). Plaster was cracked and broken on walls and ceilings, and the rear of the house, which had been servants' quarters, had no wiring, heating, or plumbing. It now accommodates an apartment upstairs, and Mrs. Minick's office below. This is Mrs. Minick's fourth restoration in Marshall; the family lived in a new house (which it disliked) for three years before coming to Oakhill. The chandeliers, love seat, desk, and blue chair are all original to the house, reupholstered and restored *(color, page 93).* The draperies are copied from those in Theodore Roosevelt's Manhattan house.

69

70

Marshall, Michigan

La Grange, Georgia

A century after it was built, this beautiful plantation house began a new life on another site (71; color, page 94). Antique buffs Betty and Kendrick Mattox were living in an 1838 house restored by his mother when they decided to move to La Grange, Georgia, to be near Mr. Mattox's business. Unable to find an old house they liked in La Grange, they brought this one with them.

The house was built in 1849 in Mrs. Mattox's home town, Grantville, Georgia, by William Glenn Arnold. It was constructed by slaves, of handmade bricks, and lumber selected by Mr. Arnold as it was brought past where he sat supervising the work. Mrs. Mattox knew and admired the house as she was growing up, but by then it had been divided into four apartments.

A fire in an upstairs bedroom had done extensive damage to part of the second floor before the Mattoxes bought it. Fortunately, they had a contractor friend who loved ante bellum houses. He agreed to move and restore it for them. He had it completely taken apart, the pieces numbered and color-coded, and stored in a warehouse until ready for reassembling.

During the course of the reconstruction they were able to install new plumbing, wiring, heating, and air conditioning, and add finer moldings and doors. They retained the original floors, windows, peg beams, and columns. The Mattoxes loved working on the restoration, enjoy living in the house, and are satisfied that the cost of moving it was no greater than building a new one.

71

Capitol Hill, Washington, D.C.

In 1957, when the Charles Ducanders bought this 1840 house in the shadow of the Capitol in Washington, D.C., it was a roach-ridden wreck. They are convinced it was being used as a brothel, because after the restoration, sailors kept knocking at their door, asking for girls by name.

When the statue of Freedom was placed atop the Capitol dome in 1865, it was made to face Capitol Hill because that was the best part of the city, where early legislators lived. But the same thing happened here as in the section of Philadelphia adjacent to Independence Hall. However, unlike Philadelphia, where an enlightened city government made use of federal programs to redeem a blighted area, Washington, the source of FHA and urban renewal funding, does nothing to assist its own neighborhood revival. On the contrary, the government demolished several blocks of Capitol Hill houses that had already been restored, and would have

destroyed others if they had not been dissuaded by homeowners and the National Trust for Historic Preservation.

Georgetown, the first urban neighborhood to renew itself, had become too expensive, so in the late 1940s and early 1950s, a few brave Washingtonians began buying houses in Capitol Hill. It has become a very lively and attractive area (72), with restoration activity growing and spreading, but when the Ducanders bought their house, it required considerable courage to invest, or even live, in the neighborhood.

Both Mr. and Mrs. Ducander worked with Congress, and were tired of the commuting problem. Mr. Ducander, from Shreveport, Louisiana, confesses that he "still gets excited" when he sees the Capitol; and the streets of Capitol Hill provide the most spine-tingling views of the dome, especially when it is illuminated at night. Though he was nervous about buying such a wretched house, he decided that the

land, so close to the Capitol, was bound to be worth the absurdly low price, even if the house could not be salvaged.

With the help of the late H. Curley Boswell, a renowned Capitol Hill restoration expert, the Ducanders transformed their house (73). They were able to save all the original floors except for those in the dining room and kitchen, where the floor is now made of Georgetown paving blocks, taken up when streetcar tracks were laid. Whatever was missing from the house was replaced by appropriate pieces of the period, such as the Louis XVI mantels, which are almost identical to those in the White House. The charming, compact little town house, with its carriage house converted to accommodate guests behind a delightful rear garden, makes an elegant setting for the Ducander's fine antique collection; and needless to say, it has proved an extremely wise investment.

New Orleans, Louisiana

New Orleans was a pioneer in preservation, passing the nation's second historic district legislation in 1936, to protect the Vieux Carré, or French Quarter. In spite of that distinction, the city has probably lost more in the last thirty years than any other city in the United States. It still has more beautiful buildings than most cities, but that is because it had so much to begin with.

The splendid procession of stately homes on St. Charles Avenue is broken by hideous commercial buildings and ugly apartment houses. The same fate has befallen Esplanade Avenue, the boulevard where Creole families built their homes. Even the prestigious Garden District has not been immune to demolition. Downtown has suffered the widest devastation, as large areas have been flattened to make way for the Superdome, and a cultural center that may never materialize. Forty per cent of the buildings in the business district (where New Orleans had a surprising number of brownstones) have been lost in the last five years. Prior to World War II, New Orleans was unable to build solid foundations for skyscrapers in its soggy ground. New technology unleashed a building rampage, changing the appearance that gave the city its distinctive charm. In the Vieux Carré, the city administration has made such an all-out effort to exploit the tourist trade that it is defeating its own purpose by gradually annihilating the very charm that brought people there in the first place.

The Vieux Carré was a residential neighborhood of fine old homes until the early twentieth century. When the French Opera House burned down in December, 1919, Lyle Saxon wrote in the *Times Picayune*, "The heart of the French Quarter stopped beating last night." The loss of this important building (where Pavlova danced, and young ladies were introduced to society) did indeed mark a turning point in the fortunes of the old quarter where the city began. Most families moved uptown, and poor Italian immigrants began living in the fine old homes, where they raised chickens, pigs, and goats, and strung clotheslines between the fanlights. Lyle Saxon was the first of many writers who found cheap living quarters in the Vieux Carré, when he bought a large old house on Madison Street in the 1930s. The Quarter became a literary center, attracting Sherwood Anderson, William Faulkner, and Oliver LaFarge as residents, and all visiting writers, who gathered at Roark Bradford's house on Toulouse Street. It was during this period (when there were no hotels, a handful of good restaurants, and few blocks of night clubs on Bourbon Street) that the Vieux Carré Commission was established to preserve the character that began to attract so many visitors. All subsequent restorations were subject to its approval.

74

Though the Vieux Carré Property Owners and Associates has been battling for years to retain its real character, the city persists in pursuing policies that are turning the French Quarter into a bawdy Disneyland, driving out long-time residents and neighborhood businesses. The latest in a series of misguided improvements was the renovation of the French Market, transforming it from a real market into a conglomeration of souvenir shops and expensive night clubs. Another disastrous city plan is a commercial sound-and-light performance in Jackson Square, and replacement of its surrounding streets with malls. The square, originally the Place d'Armes, was the military parade ground where the city of Nouvelle Orleans was born, as the Vieux Carré was built up around it, under the flags of France and Spain. Desecration of the historic square is being fought in the courts by a coalition of organizations called the Louisiana Council for the Vieux Carré.

78

The Lousiana Landmarks Society, founded in 1949, led the fight against an elevated expressway around the Vieux Carré. This proposal, promoted by the municipal government, the Chamber of Commerce, and newspapers, was defeated in 1969, after a long, desperate battle. The Society also succeeded in winning a moratorium on construction of hotels and motels in the French Quarter, and in saving and restoring the magnificent old City Hall, designed by noted architect James Gallier, now called Gallier Hall.

Another organization, Friends of the Cabildo, was formed to procure state funds for restoration of the historic Cabildo, Presbytère, Madame John's Legacy, and the old United States Mint. Friends of the Cabildo, which has become very large and active, has been publishing a series of handsome books on the city's architecture, calling attention to lost buildings and opportunities for restoration.

A typical French Quarter courtyard with characteristic rear wing and carriageway is shown here (82, 83) before and after restoration. The house and garden, severely damaged by a hurricane, remained a shambles until purchased and restored by Dr. and Mrs. Ralph Lupin.

Restoration is becoming very popular among young people, who are making attractive homes in the ubiquitous, Victorian "shotgun" (79, 80) cottages, counterparts of railroad flats, built with a series of rooms in a row. A visible change has been made in down-at-the-heels Magazine Street, adjacent to the Garden District, where a number of decrepit old houses have been converted to attractive apartments. Antique shops forced out of the French Quarter have moved into this area. Restoration has begun in the once scorned Irish Channel area, and in a depressed section near the business district, called Central City.

In the Faubourg Marigny, near the Vieux Carré, there are a growing number of restorations of the charming *petites maisons* that were homes of the mistresses of early nineteenth-century New Orleans gay blades, who gambled in the nearby casino where the game of craps was invented. These little cottages were constructed in the European manner of *briques entre poteaux,* covered with American clapboard. The Faubourg Marigny Improvement Association is preparing to fight the encroachment of a new Mississippi River bridge in the area—the same bridge that was successfully rejected first by Napoleon Avenue, then by Coliseum Square.

Though there are still many large old mansions in desperate need of restoration around Coliseum Square, luckily there were enough people involved in restoration to fight off the bridge that would have wiped it out. They won the battle by getting the entire area listed on the National Register, which prevents the use of government funds to destroy it. The petition was given special consideration because bridge

79

80

81

82

plans were going ahead, and with the help of a state agency head (who lost his job afterward), they managed to get the application through without the governor's or mayor's knowledge.

The fight was led by Duncan and Camille Strachan, pioneers in this once-fine neighborhood that had sunk to decaying rooming houses. Their house (77, 78) was built in the 1850s, and was owned by a prominent New Orleans family whom they knew, before it was taken over by a slum landlord. When they bought it in 1970, it had twelve apartments, was filled with junk and heavy machinery; the roof leaked, and plaster was falling off the walls. A forest of 150 toilet seats hung from the garage ceiling.

The Strachans began circulating a rumor that Coliseum Square was making a comeback. They knew their plan was succeeding when they began hearing the rumor themselves. Still, they thought they might live there in obscurity for years, until the bridge fight brought overnight notoriety. About thirty families moved into the neighborhood while the struggle was going on, in spite of the uncertain outcome. Though the Strachan's house is still bracketed by two large houses that appear on the verge of collapse (81), Duncan Strachan has bought several others, and is busy restoring them.

It is hard to imagine that the exceptionally fine 1867 house pictured here (74) could ever have been endangered, because it is not only beautiful, but located in the prestigious Garden District as well. However, it had been on the market for two years, and though it had never been a slum, it was in such bad condition from

neglect that everyone thought it was beyond repair. Mrs. Sam Israel, who lived in the neighborhood, had always thought it deserved to be restored. Having seen many Garden District houses in better condition being torn down, she decided she would try to do something about it.

She talked it over with her architect-brother, who warned her that it was an enormous project. He told her that they might have to tear down the rear wing, or possibly even the entire house, but if so, at least the Israels would own a fine piece of property. He also warned her that the restoration would require a good architect, a good contractor, and an owner willing to devote a year to the job.

A tremendous crack in the wall near the front door, which had frightened off potential buyers, proved not to be structural, and therefore not a major problem. In fact, interior walls were built of solid brick fourteen inches thick, all the way down to the foundations. Plumbing had been run within the rooms, plaster was stained, broken and missing, single, bare light bulbs hung on wires from the ceiling medallions. Fortunately, pieces of the elaborate plaster decoration were found in the attic, along with broken parts of the carved front door, original hardware, and the summer covers for the fireplaces, with their rare petticoat mirrors painted black.

Mrs. Israel told workmen to bring her everything they found in the house. One surprising treasure, found sealed in a wall, was an eighteenth-century French porcelain top for a commode. Even more astonishing was a human

skull with red hair, placed atop crossed thigh bones, discovered under the floorboards in the servants' quarters. This find caused much excitement and publicity. Police came and took the bones away to the coroner's office, where it was decided that they did not match. As a result, the police demanded that the contractor lift all the floor boards to search for the remainder of the skeleton. The Israels finally concluded that the bones were used for voodoo by the servants, and hidden under the floor from their masters.

Another exciting find, of far greater value, was the mural (75) on the ceiling of the dining room (originally the library). Mrs. Israel had been alerted by a local historian that there might possibly be a painting on the ceiling, so great care was taken in peeling off the wallpaper. It had been painted on canvas, in position, and was in remarkably good condition.

Two artisans spent four months skillfully restoring broken plaster decoration. Another craftsman was found to carve missing pieces of the front door. The gold valances were intact, but were cleverly extended to allow enough depth for draperies (76).

Just before work started, thieves stole the nine decorative iron oval ventilators that were set in the brick around the base of the house. Police told Mrs. Israel that they would surely be sold to stores dealing in salvage materials. After looking for two days, she found them, and had to buy them back. There was no doubt they were hers; they not only fit neatly back into the holes, but some even had traces of the house paint color on their edges.

New York, New York

Although New York City has done a thorough job of wiping out its past, there are still a few residential areas that have escaped the wrecking ball. Some blocks of houses were restored as early as the 1920s in Greenwich Village, Turtle Bay, and Sutton Place, but soaring real-estate values on the upper East Side have caused destruction of all but a few remaining pockets of early homes, for construction of high-rise apartment buildings. Luckily, much of Manhattan's West Side was spared because it was so squalid. The rows of brownstones erected as family homes in the 1880s and 1890s, were converted to rooming houses during the World War II housing shortage, and had become the refuge of the poor and the parasites—prostitutes, pimps, and addicts. If the problem had been tackled a few years sooner, the entire area surely would have been flattened by the bulldozer, but fortunately, by 1959, when an urban renewal plan was formulated for the twenty blocks between Eighty-sixth and Ninety-sixth streets, Central Park West, and Amsterdam Avenue, this kind of wholesale devastation had fallen into disfavor. Demolition of tenements and rebuilding along the major avenues was combined with rehabilitation of town houses on the side streets. Rooming houses that were not renovated by owners were taken over by the city for low-cost sale to individuals. Though new owners were required to live in their houses, to prevent the rise of a new group of absentee landlords, no architectural controls were imposed. Restoration was left to the taste and knowledge of the individual, and as a result, some houses were well done, others mutilated; some interiors were ruthlessly gutted, while others were handsomely restored. However, the overall effect was a general exterior restoration of unbroken blocks of houses which gives some idea of how the city looked in the nineteenth century. A wide variety of styles is represented, with bays, oriels, dormers, turrets, towers, and assorted roof treatments, as well as exuberant and elaborate decorative carving. An even more important effect (aside from the return of young middle-income families to live in the city) was a growing interest in restoration, which spread to the north, west, and south, leapfrogging down into Chelsea in the West Twenties, the East Village, and across the East River into Brooklyn. Shown here are two examples of handsome West Side town houses

85

86

New York, New York

(84, 86) and a detail of a typical carved wood mantel (85) from a house on Eightieth Street.

Just as Georgetown had gone into a decline after it lost its identity to Washington, so Brooklyn began its descent into stagnation, obscurity, and ridicule when it was annexed as one of the five boroughs of New York City in 1898. Yet, on its own, Brooklyn ranks as the fourth largest city in the United States, and perhaps because it has never been "developed," it still has sixteen Dutch houses, one dating to 1621, and more areas of fine nineteenth-century homes than have survived in Manhattan.

New York's wealthy businessmen began building their houses in Brooklyn when upper Manhattan was still open farm land. A ferry took them across the East River from Fulton Street in lower Manhattan to Fulton Street in Brooklyn, where they erected elegant homes on the bluff of Brooklyn Heights (87, 88). Other sites favored by millionaires were Clinton and Washington avenues in Clinton Hill, Washing-

87

88

ton Park in Fort Greene, and Park Slope along the edge of Prospect Park. All of these fine neighborhoods were abandoned after Brooklyn was annexed to New York, and Park and Fifth avenues became the fashionable places to live. All but a few wealthy families moved out. Their homes eventually became rooming houses, many boarded up during the Depression, and most streets became miserable slums.

Restoration began in Brooklyn Heights just prior to the upper West Side urban renewal in Manhattan, chiefly as a result of artists and writers seeking inexpensive living space. The Heights had a narrow escape from oblivion when its residents defeated Robert Moses's plan to build the six-lane Brooklyn-Queens Expressway diagonally across its center. The resolution of this confrontation is one of the few examples in America where a major highway not only does not intrude on the community, but enhances it. The Esplanade that was built over the completed highway (which is set into the bluff below) has become one of Brooklyn Heights's assets, a delightful promenade affording spectacular views of Manhattan's skyline. After winning this battle, citizens went on to work for enactment of New York City's landmark legislation, and Brooklyn Heights became the city's first historic district.

When houses in Brooklyn Heights became too costly, restoration spread into surrounding neighborhoods: Cobble Hill, Carroll Gardens, Boerum Hill, Park Slope, Clinton Hill, and Fort Greene. And it continues to spread and grow into still more areas. Brooklyn's chauvinism and pride in its houses is far stronger than in any Manhattan neighborhood, and this bodes well for restoration; one of the largest, proudest, and furthest advanced toward total renaissance is Park Slope (89, 90).

The streets of Fort Greene, just across the river from Manhattan, are built around a large, hilly square, originally called Washington Park, now Fort Greene Park. This was the site of a revolutionary-war fort, and a battle that George Washington lost to the British. Buried in the park is a crypt containing the bones of 11,500 soldiers, who died in captivity when they were held by the British under barbaric conditions, in old ships anchored in the harbor. Until the depression, chauffeur-driven limousines could be seen lined up in front of the grand houses along Washington Park, but in the following three decades, it disintegrated into the worst of city slums. Restoration began in the 1960s, as young urban pioneers infiltrated the grimy streets, buying rooming houses for reconversion to town houses. Though progress has been slow in the area, it will be hastened by imminent urban renewal construction nearby, as well as the revival of the adjacent business district by the Downtown Brooklyn Development Association.

The house shown here (91, 92; color, page 111), on a street off the park, was built between 1861 and 1863, and further embellished

89

90

during remodeling in 1881 by its second owner, who was a man of such prominence that the street was renamed after him. At its nadir, it was run as a rooming house by a woman who went out daily with a shopping bag peddling dope to school children. When she was arrested, dope was found hidden everywhere in the house, in heating registers, radiators, fireplaces, and every conceivable nook and cranny. After being vacant for two years, the house was bought by a young family, whose misguided renovation efforts included painting the entire stairway with yellow enamel. In 1971, discouraged by the neighborhood, they sold the house to Joseph Napoli and Robert Del Monaco, who have done an excellent restoration. Though Joseph Napoli is an English teacher, he also buys and sells antiques, and since they began work on the house, Bob Del Monaco has acquired so much salvage material from demolished Brooklyn houses that he began a sideline business selling what they cannot use. The cellar is filled with paneling, marble mantels, shutters, and ironwork, and drawers upstairs contain his remarkable private collection of hundreds of pieces of exquisitely detailed bronze hardware.

The double doors into the parlor had been removed long ago, and one of Bob's finds was a pair that fit exactly into the original opening. The parlor cornices and inlaid pier mirror, found in a Bedford-Stuyvesant house, fit the marks and slots left by the pieces that had been made for the house. All of the woodwork had been painted with false graining—*faux bois*—in fashion during the period in which the house was built. Some of it was in excellent condition—on the shutters, for instance, because they had been folded into their recesses for years. The remainder had to be restored, particularly on the stairway, after it was stripped of yellow paint. More stripping was required to restore the marble mantels, all painted at least eight times, in a spectrum of colors, each popular at a different period.

The stairway exhibits a particularly fine coffin niche: an architectural detail dictated by social custom. In the nineteenth century, the dead were laid out in the master bedroom, and when the coffin was brought down, the strategically placed niche allowed it to be maneuvered around the turn in the stairway.

Another architectural detail typical of Brooklyn houses of this period was the large, arched alcove in the master bedroom, indicating placement of the bed. In this house, the arch had to be reconstructed, because it had been plastered over to create a separate room. The bedroom cornices were found in an antique shop on Cape Cod, when Joe Napoli accidentally turned off on the wrong road. He bought them without knowing the window measurements, but they fit as if they had been made for the house.

Savannah, Georgia

Savannah is full of surprises. The infinite variety of its architecture and the leafy, green squares that interrupt the streets provide unexpected pleasures to the eye. Thanks to the unique plan of James Oglethorpe, who laid out the city in 1733, there are twenty of these urban oases, each with a different character, breaking up the regular grid of the streets. The heterogeneous quality of Savannah's architecture gives the city a noticeably less Southern feeling than Charleston, one hundred miles to the north. But like Charleston, Savannah required herculean restoration efforts to rescue the lovely city from deterioration and near oblivion.

Most of Savannah was built during the century between 1793, when Eli Whitney's invention of the cotton gin at a nearby plantation made it the capital of the cotton kingdom, and 1896, when the cotton empire collapsed. Two disastrous fires, in 1796 and 1820, wiped out most of the eighteenth-century buildings, and the builders and architects who came from the North and England to help in the rebuilding, contributed the incredible collection of architectural styles *(93, 94, 96)*. There are New England clapboards, Rhode Island gambrel roofs, Regency and Victorian row houses, and Georgian and Greek revival town houses. Unifying this living catalogue of architectural styles is Savannah's own modification: excessively high stoops *(95)* necessitated by early Savannah's sandy, unpaved streets.

The first half of the twentieth century almost destroyed what the nineteenth century had created. The entire area fell into a state of decay, with many houses becoming tenements and slums, and hundreds of others demolished. Four of the original twenty-four squares were cut for a highway that never materialized, and others had degenerated into muddy lots surrounded by chain-link fences.

The first to turn back the tide of deterioration was Mrs. Hansell Hillyer, who in 1945 converted a group of historic slum buildings near the gasworks on the river into an enclave of fifty-five dwelling units and twelve business locations. However, Mrs. Hillyer's example was not followed until almost ten years later, when the demolition of the old city market shocked citizens into organizing the Historic Savannah Foundation. At first they were just a small group of enthusiastic women, whose efforts met with disinterest from the chamber of commerce, and hostility from business groups. People were moving away from Savannah, and business leaders who wanted to attract industry felt they were trying to turn back the clock and make

94

Savannah, Georgia

the town into a museum. A few prominent businessmen joined in to help rescue the historic Davenport house, a fine Georgian home in bad condition that was slated to be demolished to provide a parking lot for a funeral home.

By 1959, the Historic Savannah Foundation had become a dynamic, well-organized group. It undertook a professional survey of some two thousand structures in the approximately two-square-mile downtown district (the historic district coincides with the financial, governmental, and cultural center, and is in fact the heart of the city), rating 1,100 buildings worthy of restoration.

Imitating Charleston's successful revolving-fund technique, Historic Savannah raised $200,000 to embark on area renovation and rescue of endangered buildings, buying and holding houses until they could be resold to individuals for restoration (a total of $1 million worth of property changed hands in this man-

ner). Sales were made with the four-point stipulation that no changes in the exterior be made without Foundation approval, the building may never be demolished, the Foundation reserves the right to buy back the building should the owner decide to sell, and restoration must begin and conclude within a given time (to discourage real-estate speculation).

In the first fifteen years of the Historic Savannah Foundation's existence, its work has been an unqualified success, with 850 to 900 of their goal of 1,100 buildings either restored or in the hands of people committed to restoration. People are buying for restoration on their own, and the city has come to recognize the economic benefits, as tourists, as well as full-time residents, are attracted to the city in increasing numbers. The tourist business increased from $1 million to $45 million, and the city has bought the old railroad station to be adapted as a visitor's center.

Dr. and Mrs. Edward Downing are an example of residents attracted to the city by its restoration activity. They had lived in New Orleans, Charleston, New York City, and London, and Dr. Downing could have practiced his profession anywhere he chose. Attracted by the 1967 *Antiques* magazine issue on Savannah, they came to look around, liked what they saw, and decided to become involved in a restoration of their own. The 1867 house they bought was one that the Historic Savannah Foundation had rescued from demolition, and when they took title in 1972, it had been vacant for eight years. An extremely large house, with a carriage house behind, it had been divided up into many apartments. Its total renovation took two years. The living room and dining room *(color, page 112)* are nobly proportioned, high-ceilinged rooms, featuring immensely tall windows to the floor, opening onto a porch across the rear of the house.

96

Richmond, Virginia

97

The Historic Richmond Foundation was formed in 1956 by a group of concerned citizens dismayed at the deterioration of the once-fine neighborhood surrounding St. John's Church. The 1741 landmark church was the site of the Virginia Convention of 1775, where Patrick Henry spoke his famous words, "Give me liberty, or give me death." On the sloping streets around the church square, high on a bluff over the James River, the city's tobacco barons built their homes in a multitude of styles, many adorned with lacy ironwork from a local foundry (97, 98). Like the early residential neighborhoods around the Capitol of the United States, and Independence Hall, Church Hill in Richmond was allowed to become a slum.

The Historic Richmond Foundation persuaded the city council to designate the area a historic district, with demolition or alteration of its buildings subject to approval by a commission of architectural review. With financial support from citizens, the organization immediately began buying and restoring houses, which in most cases were divided into several apartments for rental to young professionals. By 1958, the first restoration was completed, and by 1964, forty-one houses were restored, or in the process of restoration. As a result, young families began buying and restoring on their own, and the area has acquired renewed vitality. (Another Richmond area of later town houses, called the Fan District, is being reclaimed and renovated by individuals unaided by any organization.)

Some, who came as tenants, have remained as owners. Morris Gallagher, whose living room is pictured here, purchased the upper two floors of one of twin 1869 iron-lace-trimmed houses (99, 100) opposite the Foundation's headquarters, which are in the restored house of Edgar Allan Poe's childhood friend Elmira Shelton.

The wood-frame cottage shown here (101) is one of a pair built by carpenter John Morris in 1830, opposite St. John's Church. Their New England style, with high front stairway, is reminiscent of similar houses in Savannah.

98

99

Schenectady, New York

Scene of a bloody massacre in 1690, the Stockade district is now a peaceful and charming enclave in the industrial city of Schenectady. Its beautiful site at the confluence of the Binne Kill and Mohawk River so beguiled the Dutch that they chose to settle there in 1661 despite the dangerous proximity of hostile Indians allied with the French troops to the north. The Stockade built around their village provided very little real protection, for on a wintry night in 1690, lulled into a false sense of security, the settlers left their gates unguarded and French and Indian attackers burned the town, murdering most of its inhabitants.

Nevertheless, the stockade and houses were rebuilt, and life began anew. The Dutch were joined by English, and the town became a prosperous fur-trading center. Within twenty to thirty years there were some four hundred dwellings, and it became the northwest outpost of the American colonies, twice visited by George Washington.

In 1819, disaster struck again. Fire wiped out the wharves and warehouses along the Binne Kill, destroying many homes as well. This second tragedy may have been the salvation of the Stockade district, for commercial structures were rebuilt in a newer section of Schenectady, allowing the early settlement to survive intact as a residential neighborhood. However, in the early twentieth century, it suffered the fate that befell most American urban areas: it became a slum.

In 1932, a college professor and a lawyer bought one of the early Dutch houses in the deteriorated section, in spite of derisive comments from their friends. Though banks were unwilling to provide mortgage money, the attorney managed to obtain private financing for the purchase of several other buildings for conversion to apartments. He soon found them much in demand, as the housing shortage of World War II brought engineers hired by General Electric to rent, and then buy, houses in the area. The Stockade was launched on a program of private restoration. Quietly, without government, or outside, help of any kind, it renewed itself, and in 1962, three hundred years after its founding, it became the first historic district in New York State.

The Stockade Association was organized in 1957 to preserve and beautify the unique architecture that lines its brick-paved streets and sidewalks. It includes a score or more prerevo-

102

103

104

lutionary houses, with several Dutch houses
from the early 1700s, and at least forty-five
buildings erected prior to 1825. Later nineteenth-century houses present an evolution of
styles (104, 105, 106) through the Victorian period. Among them stand handsome early
churches (107); the 1759 St. George's Church,
and the especially beautiful 1809 Presbyterian
Church—a brick Georgian building, with grace-
ful spire and Palladian window. Throughout
the area are historical markers dating houses
and commemorating colorful events. Owners of
dated homes have bought flags representing
the periods in which their houses were built,
to be flown on holidays and special occasions.
One such occasion is the Stockade Walkabout,

an annual house tour, art show, and neighborhood festival.

The Abraham Yates house, ca. 1700, is one of
the Dutch houses rebuilt immediately following
the massacre (103). Though door and window
openings have undergone enlargement and
modification, many of its architectural features
clearly indicate its origins, particularly its steep
gable facing the street, wrought-iron beam an-
chors, and butterfly brickwork along the rake of
the gable, topped by a finial at the peak. Another notable house is the Myndert Wemple
house (102), ca. 1780. The rear of this house
may have been built as early as 1749. The Greek
revival doorway and Italianate cornice were
added during a later modification.

San Antonio, Texas

The most attractive and unique feature of San Antonio is the narrow river that meanders through the center of town (108). That river, now an asset, was formerly a menace. After severe flooding caused extensive loss of life and property damage in the early 1920s, serious consideration was given to covering it with concrete, with the bed underneath to serve as a sewer. The San Antonio Conservation Society was founded in 1924 to fight against destruction of the river.

The river was tamed with dams and other flood-control devices, and its aesthetic value enhanced to benefit the city visually and economically. A great deal of the major work was done under the WPA in 1939–41—the creation of arched bridges, broad walks, flights of steps, and attractive planting and landscaping. However, the opening of restaurants, hotels, and

businesses along the inviting walks of the narrow stream has been a more recent development. Since it was recognized as a civic asset and tourist attraction, the development of the Paseo del Rio has been guided and controlled by the River Walk Commission, established in 1962. Rehabilitation of old buildings along the riverbank has been encouraged as part of the ongoing program. Some of the successful restaurants are in early buildings that are part of La Villita, the little village that was also a WPA restoration. This block-square group of small houses of early settlers had deteriorated badly before it was restored and adapted as a display and sales center for arts and crafts, joined by attractive streets and plazas, where an annual festival is held.

The magnificent Italianate villa shown here (109) had been divided into eight dreary dwelling

units surrounded by overgrown, weed-choked grounds. It was typical of the sorry deterioration of the formerly splendid nineteenth-century homes lining the streets of the King William area of San Antonio, just south of the downtown business district. Fireplaces had been boarded up, shutters, sliding doors, and transoms nailed closed, stained-glass windows piled in a broken heap in the cellar, hand-chased, French bronze hardware caked with paint. There were ramshackle additions at the rear, and screen doors opening onto the wide interior halls.

Though his friends begged him not to, investment banker Walter Mathis decided to buy it in 1967, after his former home was demolished to make way for the North Expressway. In spite of the restoration of the nearby Edward Steves mansion as a museum in 1952, and ar-

chitect O'Neil Ford's moving his firm's headquarters into a King William Street house in 1955, there had been no appreciable improvement in the neighborhood. But Walter Mathis had enjoyed beautiful things since he was a child, buying his first antique with saved allowance when he was twelve. His restoration of this house, which began as apparent folly, became a fine investment, as completion of his own home led him to the restoration of others. Singlehandedly, he inspired the revival of the entire neighborhood.

No superficial abuse could have damaged the basic structure of this house; it was built like a fortress. Even interior walls were solid limestone. Stone masons, brought from Germany, spent two years cutting the Texas limestone and carving the acanthus-leaf decorations. Balustrades were made by the unusual method of cutting them on a lathe. The spiral stairway leading from the second floor to the tower *(112)* was constructed by carpenters on the job. Texas pine was steamed over great vats of boiling water, turned and twisted gradually, and clamped into position. The front door was specially carved in England. Four matching mantels trim the fireplaces on the ground floor, which is laid out in the ante-bellum manner; a wide central hall *(color, page 129)* separates a double parlor on one side from a triple parlor on the other.

The exterior had to be steam-cleaned to remove white paint from delicately carved stonework. The few remaining cypress shutters were repaired, and missing ones reproduced *(111)*. The nine subtly colored stained-glass windows were pieced back together, releaded, and replaced. Plasterwork was reproduced from fragments, and all rooms were repainted in their original colors. A gold-stenciled dado found under layers of paint in the downstairs reception rooms (which were all originally painted white) was carefully restored by an artist. The kitchen *(color, page 130)*, repainted in its original slate blue, features a Tiffany chandelier and an immense, handsome cabinet from a demolished mansion.

Acanthus-leaf-patterned tin shingles on the cupola were scraped down and rebuilt, and missing porch tiles replaced with matching ones from a demolished house. The fence was restored with sections of wrought iron found under the house. A curved piece of ironwork in the same pattern indicated the shape and design of the gazebo *(110)*, which has been rebuilt in the garden.

The completed house, which could not be duplicated today for a million dollars, makes an elegant showcase for Walter Mathis's exceptional collection of all sorts of fine antiques. A church-sponsored tour attracted five thousand people, and helped launch the King William area as a popular new neighborhood.

Mathis, meanwhile, restored the wreck di-rectly opposite his house. When it was completed, a handsome yellow clapboard with white Corinthian columns, he sold it to relatives. He has since bought five other houses, and spends every moment of his spare time working on restoration. He had three potential buyers for one of the houses before it was even finished.

110

Boston, Massachusetts

In 1959, Royal Cloyd lived and worked in Boston's prestigious Beacon Hill; today he lives and works in the South End, recently the city's skid row. Cloyd first saw the South End on a tour of city neighborhoods sponsored by a businessmen's luncheon club. When the tour stopped in Union Park, he got out and let the bus go on without him. He was entranced by the rows of brick, bow-front mansions, with their elaborate stone trim, carved wooden doors, and lacy ironwork balconies and stair rails (113, 114) standing in a state of mournful decay. There was a For Sale sign on one house, and he decided then and there that he would buy it. He telephoned the owner, and was quoted a price that seemed absurdly low, but when he approached his bank for a mortgage, he was greeted with absolute incredulity. The bank simply could not consider a loan on property in the South End, having lost far too much money there. Cloyd assumed they were referring to the 1929 crash, but he later learned they meant the panic of 1873!

The South End was an early example of city planning, with regular streets laid out at right angles, its rhythm occasionally varied by oval parks. By the mid-nineteenth century, it was lined with blocks of fashionable row houses, one of which was the home of J. P. Marquand's, *The Late George Apley*. The South End's heyday was brief. The panic of 1873 and the filling-in of the Back Bay brought about its downfall. Its identical row houses were overshadowed by the newly fashionable variety and richness of the Back Bay houses. So 616 acres of lavishly built Victoriana were left to decay into seedy rooming houses, and by the time Royal Cloyd arrived, the city was beginning to demolish them at the rate of two a day.

Cloyd did succeed in persuading his bank to give him a mortgage, not on the first house he planned to buy, but on another on Union Park, for which they acted as trustees. After going through the charade of a sidewalk auction at which he was the only bidder, he bought the five-story mansion for less than the house he had intended to buy. The Cloyds moved in and went to work removing partitions and restoring the two carved Italian marble mantels and ornate plaster decorations in the double parlor (115). A large party given in their new home, plus newspaper stories and television interviews, began to attract others to buy in the South End. Block associations multiplied and became the South End Federation of Citizen's Organizations, sponsoring street fairs, clean-up campaigns and house tours. Fifteen years later the South End is so well established that it suffers the usual penalty of success; real-estate prices have risen too high for private homes, and most buyers must divide their houses into several apartments.

As a result of buying the house on Union

113

114

Park, Royal Cloyd has embarked on a new career as president of the Boston Center for the Arts, a highly successful cultural center recently established in the South End. Working with the Boston Redevelopment Authority, Cloyd developed an innovative plan for the adaptive use of a group of eight old buildings, which provides low-cost, self-sustaining facilities for a broad range of artistic activities. The center gives the revived South End a focal point and offers working space for artists, while saving a substantial block of nineteenth-century buildings.

115

Chicago, Illinois

An 1880 house in Chicago illustrates how well contemporary furnishings can look in a Victorian setting (*119*). The stark, simple lines of the furniture actually dramatize and enhance the intricate detailing of carved woodwork, plaster decoration, and stained glass. The lawyer and his wife who bought this house when it was divided to accommodate fourteen roomers, worked diligently to restore ornamental plaster and strip the woodwork that was caked with paint (*118*). Doing much of the work themselves, they saw the history of the house unfold as they peeled back layers of carpeting and linoleum. Between each successive layer were newspapers: the first was 1945, then 1920, 1900, and finally, 1890. Paint colors for the walls were adopted from the multi-hued nineteenth-century ceramic tiles in the floor of the vestibule.

This house is in the Mid-North district of Chicago, part of the Lincoln Park Conservation Association, a confederation of seven old residential neighborhoods, just north of the Loop. It borders on Lincoln Park, on the shore of Lake Michigan. Except for a handful of cottages that escaped the ravages of the Great Fire, all of its homes postdate 1871. Though there are a few rows of matching houses, most blocks are a riot of architectural styles, predominantly variations of Italianate, Queen Anne, and Richardsonian Romanesque—interspersed with Chicago's own cottage style. This unique form, somewhat incongruous in a skyscraper city, was a pre-fire development—a simple, pitched-roof cottage, gable end facing the street, with an extremely high stairway from the front door to the sidewalk. The evolution of this high-stoop style was a result of flooding, and the fact that the street level was constantly being raised.

The entire area had fallen into slum condition, as, in the usual pattern, its residents deserted it for newly fashionable suburbs. Revival began in the 1940s in Old Town, with artists and writers seeking inexpensive living space. Old Town's successful renaissance spread to adjoining neighborhoods, encompassing two square miles and more than seventy thousand people. By 1956, the city designated Lincoln Park a conservation area. The Lincoln Park Conservation Association, which represents the entire area, is a commendably strong, active organization that encourages authentic restoration. It has been extremely vigilant and remarkably successful in legal action against developers who try to erect high-rise buildings among its tree-shaded blocks of nineteenth-century houses (*116, 117*).

River Forest, Illinois

Frank Lloyd Wright seems so much a twentieth-century architect that it is somewhat surprising to associate his work with restoration. Yet Wright had already served his apprenticeship with Louis Sullivan, and had been working on his own for more than ten years by the time he designed this house in 1901. The Oak Park and River Forest suburbs of Chicago are a treasure trove of early Frank Lloyd Wright; this house in River Forest is just a few blocks away from a score of other homes he designed, as well as his own home and studio in Oak Park, which also needs restoration.

A comparison of the 1890s high Victorian style (well-represented in Chicago's Lincoln Park area) with Wright's work executed at the same time, makes very clear what a shocking innovator he must have seemed. And the value in having real examples of these simultaneous building styles as illustrations of architectural and social history is a testament to the importance of historic preservation.

Though this house, built for E. Arthur Davenport, had only three owners, it had fallen into sorry condition through neglect. The garage was near collapse, the house gutters and downspouts were full of holes, which caused damage to the cedar board-and-batten exterior; glass was broken in some of the windows, and the seventy-year build-up of paint and wallpaper was beginning to part company with the walls.

Just as the For Sale sign was going up, Jeannette Fields came looking for a Frank Lloyd Wright house. The Fieldses needed to move because Mr. Fields's business was relocating. Mrs. Fields, who had always been an architectural buff, knew about the many Wright houses in the suburbs, though she had never seen them. So she called a realtor and asked if there were any on the market. He knew of the Davenport house, but because of its bad condition, he tried to sell her something else. The moment she saw it, she wanted to buy it.

The house clearly shows the Japanese influence that so strongly affected Wright, and abounds in the special features of his distinctive style. It is built in a cruciform plan, with characteristic low ceilings and spaces that flow into each other. It has nearly black stained beams and woodwork, built-in furniture (including the fireplace inglenook), and almost jewel-like windows (121, 122). The entrance, hidden from sight from the street, is at ground level, covered with a low roof (120). Inside is the sudden surprise of vertical openings on either side of the stairway, and making the most of the compact interior, a turn is required before entry into the living room. Jeannette Fields describes the living room as dramatic—a spiritual, emotional experience. "He left nothing to chance; the way the light comes in, the way you look from one space into another." She concedes that Wright's strong personality dominates and dictates lifestyle and furnishings and it forced her to get rid of most of her old furniture.

By coincidence, or fate, the Fieldses bought the Wright house in the same year, 1970, that her lifelong interest in architecture brought her an exciting new job as director of the Chicago School of Architecture Foundation, where she introduced their highly successful tour program. It is the only program of its kind in the country, offering a wide variety of architectural tours to the public, making them see buildings they had never noticed.

121

124

Cape May, New Jersey

Cape May, discovered by Henry Hudson and established as a Dutch colony and whaling center in 1632, became a seaside resort after the war of 1812. It may be America's oldest resort, and at its peak in the second half of the nineteenth century, was rivaled only by Newport, Rhode Island, Saratoga Springs, New York, and Long Branch, New Jersey. It was superseded by Atlantic City in the early twentieth century, and suffered a decline.

Fires destroyed many of the wood-frame buildings; there were two particularly disastrous ones in 1867 and 1878, with the latter wiping out thirty acres. The lacy, fanciful houses and hotels that remained were considered hopelessly old fashioned until the awakening of interest in nostalgia in the 1960s. Since then there has been a concerted effort towards preservation and restoration.

Both the 1879 Pink house (123) and the Star Villa, one of Cape May's several picturesque hotels, had to be moved to escape demolition. The Pink house was converted to an antique shop, becoming part of the new Washington Street shopping complex. Though Cape May's distinctive buildings have been thoroughly documented for the National Register, many problems must be overcome to assure their future maintenance. Local bankers and politicians have been blind to their value, denying financing and overriding urban renewal plans and controls; and the large rambling old hotels desperately need modernizing to remain viable. However, preservationists, led by dedicated Carolyn Pitts of Philadelphia, are determined to win their battle for the restoration of these delightful confections of Victorian woodwork (124, 125).

123

Key West, Florida

Key West was settled in 1822 by merchants and manufacturers, but as in Cape May, none of the earliest houses remain owing to two major fires. There has been further loss in the twentieth century to hurricanes and termites, and demolition of buildings on the main street for replacement by stores.

Old Island Restoration was organized in the 1960s; prior to that, people took the older houses for granted, and one neglected historic house was lost by fire. In the last five years there has been a growing interest in preservation. The Audubon House (a ship pilot's house, visited by Audubon) was restored as a museum; warehouses in the old dock area were converted to a theater, community center, and other public use; and there has been an increase in private restoration (126).

126

Georgetown, Washington, D.C.

Georgetown is widely known as the prestigious address of Washington's elite, home of statesmen and legislators, where young Senator John F. Kennedy lived before he was elected to the Presidency. Millions of visitors admire its delightful tree-shaded streets, brick sidewalks, and rows of lovely town houses (127, 128). Few people realize that this elegant enclave in the nation's capital, this prototype of the sophisticated city neighborhood, was a slum in the early 1930s.

Established as a tobacco port in 1751, Georgetown was one of the most important shipping centers of the colonial period, home of prosperous merchants and landowners. Pierre L'Enfant lodged in a Georgetown tavern while devising his famous plan for the city of Washington, which at that time, was only muddy, undeveloped land. However, after Washington became America's capital, it swallowed up Georgetown. Congress revoked its right to a separate government, and the use of its name, robbing it of its identity. Even its distinctive street names were changed to conform with the District of Columbia's alphabetical system.

Though it had its ups and downs in the nineteenth century, the ultimate decline of Georgetown began with the Civil War, and by the early twentieth century, all but a few families had deserted their town houses for the newly fashionable suburbs. Most of the area was so run-down that the family and friends of the first young people who bought houses there in the 1930s thought they had taken leave of their senses; and bank financing was, of course, denied to them.

They had come to Washington to work in Franklin D. Roosevelt's New Deal administration, and in the bleak years following the depression, few could afford the price of a home in the suburbs. So they discovered Georgetown, with its wonderful variety of town houses, large and small, in styles ranging from Federal to Victorian. What followed was a kind of benevolent epidemic. After one family transformed a depressing, grimy wreck into a trim, smartly manicured town house, there was a contagious reaction. Friends and acquaintances became

imitators, and a snowballing effect reversed the tide of blight on block after block. Property values skyrocketed, and the first investors were able to reap large profits, if they so desired. The highly successful, spontaneous restoration of Georgetown became a symbol, inspiring countless other neighborhood revivals that began in the 1940s and 1950s in cities throughout the country.

Georgetown's only problem today is coping with a surfeit of success. An estimated fourteen million tourists a year invade its one square mile; sidewalk vendors and excessive traffic snarl its commercial center. Developers are finding means to get around the laws protecting old buildings by allowing them to deteriorate until they are beyond restoration. Homeowner groups, such as the Citizens Association of Georgetown, are working on controlling these hazards to the preservation of their community.

The 1853 Herron-Moxley house is one of the large-scale Georgetown homes that survived rather well through Georgetown's period of decline. However, even some of those suffered a sorry fate. The nearby home of Senator Claiborne Pell, an earlier house that was visited by many famous statesmen, was used for years as a warehouse, earning the nickname "haunted house," and requiring extensive restoration. The Herron-Moxley house was twice sold for unpaid taxes, and was the subject of liens for twenty-five years. It was originally built as a farm, surrounded by barn, ice house, and carriage house; its land encompassed the entire block. Not only had the other land and buildings been whittled away, but the house itself was threatened with demolition by a developer in the mid-1960s. He was stopped by the Fine Arts Commission.

The house was bought by the Charles Fenwicks in 1969. It was in run-down condition, with cracked ceilings, and floors studded with nails from wall-to-wall carpeting. The house had been extensively altered and Victorianized in an earlier period, and Mrs. Fenwick found the dark woodwork and heavy black marble mantels excessively gloomy. She replaced the mantels with earlier ones, found for her by restoration expert H. Curley Boswell, and brightened the large, handsome rooms and gleaming floors. Long windows opening onto tree-shaded porches provide a country atmosphere for this city house in Georgetown (*color, page 147*).

Georgetown, Washington, D.C.

Georgetown, Colorado

Georgetown has begun a third lease on life. Its first incarnation was extremely brief, as the gold discovered there by prospector George Griffith (the town was named after him) petered out within a year or two. Its real boom began in 1864 in rich silver mines, and continued until the repeal of the Sherman Silver Act in 1893, when the plummeting price of silver ruined many a western mining town. During its three-decade heyday, Georgetown became a major Colorado city, with a population of five thousand, two opera houses, two newspapers, several luxurious hotels, five churches, five firehouses, and many saloons. In 1884, the Georgetown Loop was completed—an engineering feat involving four and a half miles of elevated railway track looping back over itself on high trestles, to enable trains to climb six hundred feet up to Silver Plume in the mountains above Georgetown.

After the 1893 crash, Georgetown's population dwindled to two hundred by the 1930s. Many of its abandoned buildings deteriorated and were demolished. But Georgetown began a third life in the economic boom following World War II, as its lovely mountain setting and easy access to Denver (forty-six miles away) made it an ideal site for leisure homes.

However, unlike Aspen, Georgetown is determined to control its revival so that its Victorian charm is not buried under haphazard new building and overdevelopment. A plan by the state of Colorado to rebuild the Georgetown Loop so that tourists can see how silver was mined will certainly send Georgetown real-estate prices skyrocketing. Georgetown, Colorado, will have to battle, just as Georgetown in Washington, D.C. is now battling, to survive in the face of excessive popularity. The Georgetown Historical Society is already involved in a court fight to prevent the incursion of condominiums.

Meanwhile, the whole town is being restored. In 1966, the Georgetown Silver Plume mining district was designated a national historic landmark, and a number of Georgetown buildings were listed on the National Register. In 1970, an historic preservation ordinance was passed, and the Georgetown Historical Society was formed.

Hamill house, with its majestic rear office and coach-house buildings, iron fountain, and elaborate cupola-topped, crested privy (130), is being meticulously restored as a museum. The Hotel de Paris, an elaborate Norman hostelry built by a Frenchman, was opened as a museum after it ceased operating as a hotel in 1954. Maxwell house, restored as a private home, is regarded as one of the ten finest Victorian houses in the United States (color, page 148). The hundred-year-old Star Hook and Ladder building, its bell retrieved and its shield painstakingly reconstructed, has been restored to a new life as the town offices and playhouse (129) for a local dramatic group. The main street boasts a fine row of typical false-front western commercial buildings, housing a handsome bank and a fine restaurant.

129

130

San Francisco, California

Though nineteenth-century San Francisco houses were an eclectic mixture of every conceivable style, the resulting architecture is unique and unmistakable. A wonderful variety of exuberant, whimsical millwork made up of assorted brackets, fretwork, fans, scallops, dentils, and curlicues decorates towers, bays, turrets and loggias; with cornices crowning façades that often extend well above the houses they adorn (*131, 132, 133, 134*).

The sheer visual delight of this marvelous architectural heritage was not generally recognized until the redevelopment agency wiped out 5,000 houses in the late 1950s and early 1960s in a misguided program of urban renewal in the Western Addition. (There are only about 2,500 of these buildings remaining today.) The tragic loss provoked cries of outrage, and made San Franciscans aware of the irreplaceable value of these rare houses. It also made them realize that preservation was essential if they were to retain the special quality of their city.

Unlike most stone Victorians, or simpler early wood clapboards, these houses present more of a restoration challenge on the exterior than on the interior. It is a challenge that few homeowners or contractors are equipped to handle. For not only had homes deteriorated

through lack of maintenance, but the even worse scourge of modernization had destroyed or mutilated many façades. Salesmen still sweep through neighborhoods, leaving in their wake a blight of Permastone, and asbestos and aluminum siding. There is even a new, horrible development called Texcote, a sprayed-on layer of stucco with hair!

To repair the damage, a new company called San Francisco Victoriana was established in 1973. The very fact that there is enough need for a business devoted solely to the restoration of Victorian houses is in itself an encouraging sign. It began when four young men who met in the army decided to combine their talents, took a loan from the Small Business Administration, and set up shop. They have been very busy ever since. Working from a collection of rare old catalogues, they soon became expert at duplicating missing parts or recreating entire façades of San Francisco Victorians. Their millwork is fabricated only from redwood (as were the originals), which is impervious to rot, mildew, or insects. Everything they reproduce has to equal the quality of the original, though they somehow manage to keep prices at a reasonable level. They insist on authenticity and the highest standards in the millwork and hardware

132

San Francisco, California

133

they manufacture, as well as in the ornamental plaster and beveled, etched, and stained glass that they have made by other local craftsmen.

While San Francisco Victoriana is repairing the damage, San Francisco Heritage is fighting to prevent the need. This group, similar to historic foundations in other cities, is working with a revolving fund to purchase and resell endangered buildings, with protective easement clauses added to the deeds in perpetuity as preservation for the future.

Though there are Victorian houses scattered throughout the city, the most active restoration is in the Mission district, the oldest residential neighborhood surviving the disastrous 1906 earthquake and fire. Like the largely demolished Western Addition, the Mission district became a refuge for low-income families after World War II, and as a result, its population is diverse. To solve neighborhood problems and obtain Model Cities funds and home improvement loans, the Mission Coalition Organization was founded. An outgrowth of this organization was the Victorian Alliance, promoting appreciation, restoration and preservation of Victorian façades, and fighting to change zoning and tax laws that make maintenance of older homes difficult. Having proved effective in the Mission district, the Victorian Alliance is branching out into other neighborhoods with vulnerable Victorians, such as Alamo Square, Duboce Triangle, Eureka and Noe valleys, Buena Vista, Haight Ashbury, and Haight Fillmore.

In the Mission district, restoration is often carried out by young people on a do-it-yourself basis. For instance, one family bought a derelict building to house a second-hand clothing boutique. There were weeds growing in the refuse piled inside the building; the previous owner had felt that it should be torn down for a parking lot. For nearly two years, the couple and their children spent evenings and weekends restoring the house, hauling out rubble and stripping five coats of enamel off the stairway. After the shop opened in 1967, they responded to the opportunity to rescue another house two doors away. No sooner had they completed the second restoration and rented it, than they took on the center house, making three in a row. This is not affluent, prestige restoration carried out by architects and contractors, but primarily young, middle-class professionals recognizing and reviving the quality of a bygone era. Their industry is clearly evident in the brightly painted, fanciful façades once more gracing the streets of San Francisco.

Covington, Kentucky

The nineteenth-century houses set amongst gardens, lawns, and trees on Riverside Drive in Covington, Kentucky, face downtown Cincinnati across the Ohio River—another state, another world. But this bucolic community has had to fight for its life against urban redevelopment. In 1969, when Covington's city commissioners tried to turn the area over to developers for an apartment-hotel-office complex, residents defeated the move, and had the area designated an historic district.

A more recent confrontation involves construction of a new bridge, which would necessitate destroying the 1874 Hearne house. Questioning the need for another bridge, and maintaining that the Hearne house serves as an

entranceway into the Riverside district, residents blocked demolition by getting the house listed on the National Register, which prevents the use of federal funds for its destruction. If it is saved, the Hearne house is in great need of restoration, but restoration is becoming contagious in this Kentucky town on the Ohio and Licking rivers. Covington had been largely written off for twenty years, as affluent residents moved out to surrounding suburbs. John Kunkel and Richard Smith were the first to begin buying large old houses there in the mid-1960s, and now own several, including the important Carneal house (135).

Carneal house was built in 1815 by Thomas Carneal, a founder of Covington. The first brick house in the city, this Georgian-Palladian mansion was visited by Lafayette in 1825; other distinguished guests included Henry Clay, Daniel Webster, and Andrew Jackson. A vaulted stone tunnel leading from the basement to the bank of the Licking River is reputed to be the last stop on the Underground Railway, though the owners doubt it. The house, which had been altered, was in deteriorating condition when Kunkel and Smith bought it. They have converted it into large, handsome apartments. Across the street another impressive house, the

1865, French Victorian, Laidley house (137) is being restored and converted to luxury apartments by a doctor and his wife, who have also bought two other houses nearby. Next door to the Laidley house, on the corner facing the Carneal house, is a majestic brick mansion with soaring Corinthian columns (138). Built in 1865 as a Tuscan villa, with a three-story tower in the rear, it was modified to Greek revival with the addition of the columned portico, at the turn of the century. After being left vacant for ten years, it was recently sold to Dean Howe, who had previously restored houses in New York City and Franklin, Ohio. Though all of its plumbing and heating had been rendered useless by frozen, burst pipes, miraculously, its magnificent interiors escaped serious damage. Howe means to restore them meticulously, including the delicately painted ceilings, lacy moldings and medallions, woodwork and paneling, and original wallpaper.

Though the Riverside area of Covington has attracted many restorers and renovators, few had ventured into the downtown area, where the neighborhood is seedier and the streets are marred with typical twentieth-century pollution —ugly new buildings and hideous signs. Recently, however, law partners Paul Vesper and Ed Wintherberg bought an exceptionally handsome town house just in time to prevent its being sold for demolition to make a parking lot. They have adapted the building as law offices, making almost no changes in its interior. They restored the lovely long parlor as a library-conference room, regilding the elaborate plaster decoration on its high ceiling. The stone façade has been cleaned, and paint stripped from the beautifully carved front doorway with its high-relief medallions. Their sensitive adaptation is opposite a glaring example of the worst in urban ugliness: another old building converted to an automobile sales office sporting a huge, garish neon sign and large, unsightly winged fluorescent lights.

Another downtown pioneer is Charles Eilerman, who has made up for his late entry into Covington's restoration activity by becoming its most fervent supporter. Eilerman began by buying the Grant house in 1973, to save it from demolition (136). The home of Ulysses S. Grant's parents, built in 1850, it had deteriorated into a fifteen-unit rooming house, full of filth, roaches, and bats. In a short time, Eilerman removed the tacked-on front porch, cleaned up and repaired the exterior, and made the two-family Grant house into three spacious apartments. Though he invested a great deal of money in saving the house, there has been no increase in rental income since it was a tenement. Undaunted, he bought two more houses, and leaped into the forefront of the battle to save the Hearne house from demolition, thereby sacrificing the good will of the banker whose mortgage enabled him to buy the Grant house.

137

Introduction

Private enterprise and progress have always been regarded as sacred to the American ethic. Progress is synonymous with newness; *ipso facto,* nothing old must be allowed to stand in the way of anything new. Thousands of beautiful buildings, created with grandeur of style, fine materials and workmanship, providing an irreplaceable link with the past, have been sacrificed without a qualm to the right of individuals to exploit our land for profit. Intoxicated with our apparently boundless resources, our throwaway society has never paused to consider the waste. The energy crisis, and the shocking realization that America's wealth is indeed finite, must make us stop and re-evaluate our priorities. Should we continue to allow private profit to reign supreme, destroying fine, useful buildings in order to overcrowd our landscape with energy-wasting, often unneeded, and monotonous skyscrapers that violate our skylines and reduce human beings to an army of ants? Even some architects have begun to say no.

Though architects have traditionally demanded the right to express their creative abilities in designing new buildings, effective re-use of an old building can be equally challenging. With a positive attitude, and enough time and determination, it is usually feasible to adapt an old building for a profitable and productive new life. Recycling of Boston's old City Hall (a prime example cited by the American Institute of Architects in a remarkable advertisement in *Time* magazine promoting adaptive use) is a case in point. A blue-ribbon panel appointed by Boston's mayor declared preservation of the building financially impossible, and yet a way was found to save it that proved both practical and praiseworthy.

Regressive real-estate tax policies must be revised to encourage rehabilitation rather than reward property owners who allow buildings to deteriorate or, even worse, demolish them in order to escape taxation. Legislation must be amended to eliminate the sort of wasteful policies that can contribute to the destruction of an important building such as the one designed by Richard Morris Hunt in 1881 as a home for the elderly on the upper West Side of Manhattan. This building, considered one of the most gracious and comfortable homes for the aged in the country, was the only significant structure in the midst of a mass of mediocre high-rise housing. One of the few surviving Hunt buildings in New York, it was the sole visible anchor to the past remaining in the neighborhood. Less than a decade after it was remodeled—in 1965, at a cost of $500,000—it failed to meet new fire-safety regulations. New York State agreed to fund $10 million for new construction, but would not consider expenditure of $5 million for renovation of this magnificent nineteenth-century structure to meet the required standards. The new building would accommodate more people, but with a loss of privacy, human amenities, and a delightful enclosed garden. Once more we are prepared to waste a fine structure to replace it with a shoddy, banal substitute that costs twice as much. Clearly, governmental policy must change, and aroused public opinion is the only means of changing it.

We have always been too quick to bow to the will of the property owner, who, in his eagerness to erect another structure that will allow him to milk every last penny from every inch of real estate, assures us that whatever occupies the space is obsolete, impractical, and expendable. (The architecturally significant Chicago Stock Exchange was sacrificed in 1971 as "economically unviable," to make way for an undistinguished new skyscraper which was in serious financial difficulty less than four years later.) According to our ethos, his right to make the highest possible profit from that piece of land supersedes all other considerations. Although we are beginning to look for compromises, owners are not compelled to accept them —as perhaps they should be. The Penn Central, offered another site on which to build, preferred to take the city of New York to court in its determination to abrogate the landmarks law and destroy Grand Central Station.

Library, Portland, Maine (opposite)

Ghirardelli Square, San Francisco, California

Not all recycling is automatically good. Sometimes we must ask: Which is worse, inappropriate re-use or total demolition? A church recycled as a supermarket, another transformed into a discotheque called The Sanctuary, might give pause to the most ardent preservationist. Would it be preferable to lose the building, or accept a compromise in the hope that the structure's continuing existence might eventually lead to a better solution?

Architects cannot be held solely responsible for bad adaptive use. Owners often demand an approach that precludes innovative design. Such a case is the plan proposed for the landmark Villard houses, which have the misfortune of standing on prime mid-Manhattan real estate. Landmark laws can prevent destruction only if an economically viable solution agreeable to the property owner can be devised. The archdiocese of New York, owner of the Villard houses, has contracted to lease the property to a real-estate company that proposes to erect a high-rise hotel on the site. The plan submitted to the Landmarks Commission abuses, rather than re-uses the existing buildings, and yet the Commission could be compelled to accept it, or risk razing of this important, U-shaped group of town houses. Rather than incorporating the beautiful nineteenth-century interiors into the ground floor of the new hotel, the plan would demolish all but the façade of the center building, which will be used as the entrance to an unrelated, inappropriate skyscraper—with a lobby decorated in the "style" of the demolished building. Re-use of the remaining wings of the Villard houses is left unresolved. While, admittedly, the situation is not entirely equivalent, it is interesting to compare this abortive plan to the San Domenico in Taormina, Sicily, a renowned luxury hotel created in a fourteenth-century convent. The dramatic character of the architecture, retained, rather than violated, is basic to the special quality that makes the hotel superior.

In point of fact, investors, developers, and property owners should be made to realize that wherever existing structures have been imaginatively and sensitively adapted, they have attracted praise, prizes, and profit.

The public is becoming more and more prone to protest demolition of favorite buildings, and to show appreciation for responsible restoration. Fifty-five thousand San Franciscans signed petitions against Neiman Marcus's proposed destruction of the City of Paris department store. The president of the Merchants National Bank in Winona, Minnesota, was shocked when citizens reacted negatively to his lovely plans for a new building to replace the 1912 bank. There were so many letters of protest (from as far away as California, and even Rome) that the board of directors reversed its decision, restoring and modernizing the old bank instead of building a new one. They were rewarded with prizes, commendations, streams of visitors, and even transferral of funds from competing banks by appreciative members of the community.

The Cleveland Trust Company was threatened with removal of substantial accounts if they tore down their turn-of-the-century neoclassic headquarters. The Rookery in Chicago, the Chandler Building in Atlanta, Carnegie Hall in New York City, and the Academy of Music and Pennsylvania Academy of Fine Arts in Philadelphia, have all been restored and modernized. The inherent character of the commercial buildings has proved effective in attracting tenants, while new office towers remain half empty. And Carnegie Hall, which was nearly torn down when its replacement was built in Lincoln Center, is engaged by many orchestras that prefer it to its successor.

More and more old buildings that would have been demolished a decade ago are being adapted and put back to work to serve new purposes. Many of these buildings have irreplaceable architectural and historical value that can be restored on the exterior even if the interior must be altered. But they need not be of landmark quality to be worth recycling. As a recent

New York Times editorial noted, "Good old buildings of any kind are being looked at as an untapped resource . . . represent[ing] materials, techniques and styles that will never be seen again." Such structures provide important stability and character to a neighborhood, and their destruction can represent a very real loss.

Some adaptive use of old buildings has been going on for a very long time, such as the conversion of barns and coach houses to homes. Many of the mammoth mansions of the wealthy, built to be maintained by hordes of servants, have been salvaged for use as schools, consulates, and embassies. But today, as many mourn the loss of Pennsylvania Station and the Metropolitan Opera House, and scores of railroad stations and churches stand idle for lack of trains and worshippers, adaptive use is becoming an obvious alternative to costly new construction.

The number and variety of railroad stations in America staggers the imagination; architects indulged the kind of creativity in designing railroad stations that their predecessors had lavished on cathedrals. Some obsolete stations have already been redesigned for other functions, smaller ones as homes or shops, and larger ones to serve a multitude of purposes: a bank in Lincoln, Nebraska, a visitors' center in Washington, D.C., a transportation terminal and shopping complex in Indianapolis, Indiana, and a restaurant and hotel (with Victorian suites in antique Pullman cars) in Chattanooga. The fate of scores of others hangs in the balance.

As nostalgia sweeps the country, recycling of old buildings is being recognized as good business. A national restaurant chain is based on the use of old railroad cars, signs, and equipment; and banks and churches have been successfully converted to restaurants, with all their special features played up as an attraction to customers. The craze for stained glass, wood, and ironwork, and anything reminiscent of the "good old days" can be emphasized, or incorporated, in re-using an old structure. A block of nineteenth-century buildings, left behind when the street level was raised in Atlanta, was rediscovered and turned into an area of night clubs, bars, and cafes called Underground Atlanta, immediately winning national fame. The Crystal Palace, a popular Aspen, Colorado, supper club in an old commercial building with a carefully preserved White Owl Cigar sign painted on its outside wall, uses wood mantels as a base for its bar, iron bedsteads for balcony railings, and acres of stained glass hung on walls and ceilings.

On the other hand, the large interior spaces provided by old nonresidential buildings can accommodate imaginative contemporary interiors without destruction of exterior integrity. Large spaces as well as low costs are usually the chief factors that tempt people to make their homes in stables or churches instead of conventional houses that are divided into rooms. Although it used to be regarded as eccentric, today there is even a certain cachet, or status, in dwelling in a converted building.

Ghirardelli Squire (*page 162*) on San Francisco Bay has been as important an influence on large-scale adaptive use as Georgetown was in the restoration of declining residential neighborhoods. The phenomenal success of this unlikely group of old factory buildings as a shopping-entertainment-restaurant complex has inspired countless imitators: The Cannery and Jackson Square in San Francisco, Larimer Square in Denver, Pioneer Square in Seattle, Trolley Square in Salt Lake City, Canal Square in Georgetown, Washington, D.C., as well as more loosely defined areas, such as the Old Port Exchange in Portland, Maine, and the waterfront warehouses converted to boutiques in Alexandria, Virginia. An old torpedo factory in Alexandria was recently remodeled as an art center accommodating 130 private studios, 5 workshops, and 3 galleries. The Boston Center for the Arts is made up of a group of eight assorted

Aspen, Colorado (opposite)

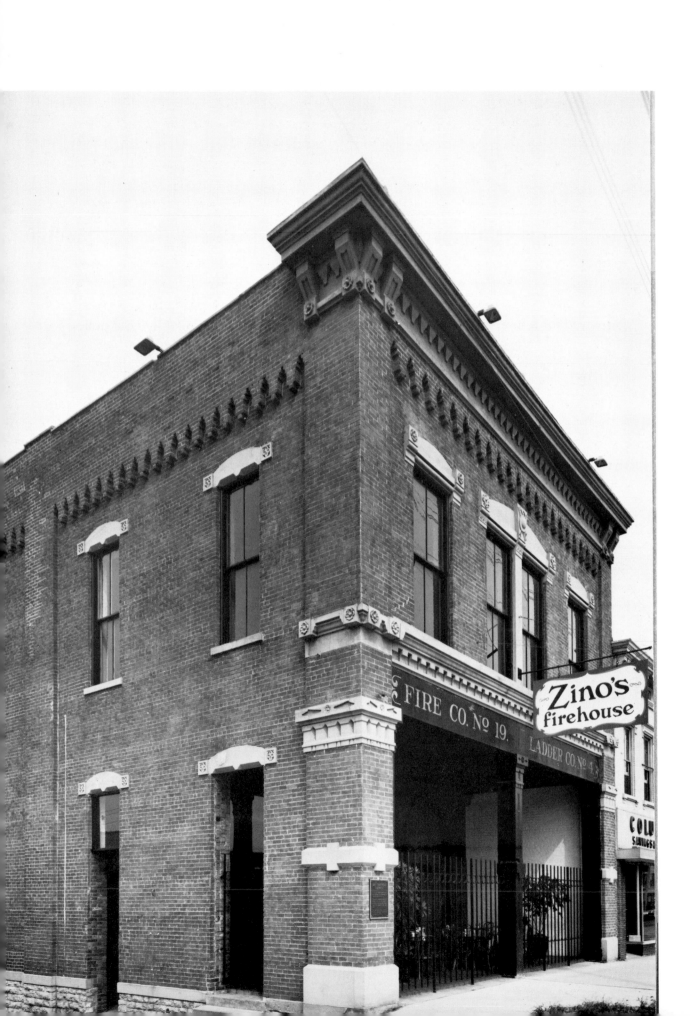

buildings, including a piano factory, a parking garage, a gasoline station, an apartment house, and a theater.

Scores of huge, incredibly elaborate movie palaces erected in the heyday of Hollywood and vaudeville had already been razed when Powell Symphony Hall inspired a succession of imitators of its conversion of the old St. Louis Theater. A few years ago, Americans would never have considered salvaging these white elephants, twentieth-century architecture revered by no one. The recent past is almost never respected. We wiped out much of our Victoriana before we began to appreciate it. What a shame it would have been to erase all trace of these magnificent cinema castles of the 1920s and 1930s. But there are more practical reasons for the rescue of the St. Louis Theater and those that have followed it: superior acoustics, enormous financial savings, and a splendid setting for concerts.

All obsolete federal government buildings were routinely demolished by law until public pressure demanded the rescue of the St. Louis post office. New legislation had to be passed (since called the St. Louis Post Office Act) to put an end to this wasteful practice, allowing federal buildings to be recycled. There is a growing list of city government structures that have been saved for re-use: New Orleans's and Boston's old city halls, New York City's old police headquarters and extravagantly elaborate Customs House, among others. Their beauty, character, and scale provide sorely needed variety and contrast to the unbroken, sheer vertical walls of steel, concrete, and glass that surround them.

Fortunately, there are so many examples of adaptive use all over America today that it is impossible to represent them in depth. Westbeth in New York City, a huge telephone-company building, was converted to artists' apartments, studios, and galleries, and the Chickering Piano Factory in Boston was similarly converted. A Jersey City bank has been transformed into apartments, and so has a Portland, Maine, school. A church, also in Portland, Maine, has become a library (*page 160*). In Cincinnati, Ohio, an 1871 firehouse was converted into an attractive pizza restaurant (*page 166*), whose design won an American Institute of Architects award. And an important department store in New York City has recently been commercially adapted to rental units with resulting acclaim and admiration. Several of New Orleans's finest restaurants are in former homes, and Aspen, Colorado, is a riot of adaptive use (*page 165*).

The explosion of recycling across America makes the choice of examples extremely difficult. All those shown in the following pages are well-designed adaptations of buildings worth saving. Their success makes important points architecturally, historically, socially, and economically. They speak for themselves.

Pizza restaurant, Cincinnati, Ohio (opposite)

Church, Bellport, New York

This church has had a checkered career since it was built in 1848 in Bellport, Long Island. A Methodist-Episcopal church until 1946, it was changed to Presbyterian, and then replaced in 1961, when the community purchased and moved a 1740 church from South Haven. It was being used as an all-purpose meeting hall when mural painter Philip Read bought it for a home and studio in 1964. When Read happened to go through the town on his way to the Hamptons, he fell in love with its quiet "Norman Rockwell scene" and went to a real-estate broker to inquire about a house. The church was the only building for sale. Though he has now owned it for a decade, people from the community who think it is still theirs are likely to walk in, look around, and reminisce. When he first bought it,

he was inside sweeping when a bus drove up, a group of boys in band uniforms marched in, tuned up, and began practicing. He assumes they thought he was the janitor. They played for an hour, marched out, and drove away.

More recently, after he completed the renovation, he was sitting with friends having cocktails when a couple with cameras around their necks walked in exclaiming, "What a lovely old church!" Unperturbed, Read takes it all in good humor.

The church (139) works beautifully for Read. He did not have much money when he bought it, and could not have afforded to buy this kind of space in a conventional house. There was no running water, plumbing, kitchen, or bathroom, and the floors were in bad condition where the

pews had been nailed down. He did the renovation gradually over three or four years, with the help of workmen from the town. Structural changes were minimal; he created two rooms by walling in both sides of the former altar, and did some work on the cellar to turn it into a kitchen and dining room.

In spite of its elegant appearance, the interior decor (140) is made up more of ingenuity than money. Cut-down pews have become chairs; the coffee table is the former framed-glass, church notice board set on pipe legs; and most of his furnishings were bought from Long Island farms and junk shops. Altogether, this is an effective example of total adaptive use and recycling.

139

Bakery, Philadelphia, Pennsylvania

Though exterior restoration is strictly controlled in Philadelphia's Society Hill to conform with the eighteenth-century architecture of William Penn's colony on the Delaware River, interiors contain a wide variety of styles. In nearly two hundred years of use and abuse, many of the buildings were altered so drastically that little remained to be restored. Some of these houses have been gutted and remodeled in starkly dramatic contemporary style. The house bought by architect Adolf de Roy Mark (142), directly opposite the Ingersoll house shown on page 62, was built in 1802 as the home and shop of a baker. The lower portion of the façade, which originally contained a store front, was in such bad condition that it had to be completely reconstructed. The interior, which was also in terrible shape, lent itself to the sort of treatment that Mark enjoys designing: contemporary space enhanced and warmed by the use of old materials. He not only uses everything that can be saved in a house, but adds pieces he collects or salvages, such as woodwork, glass, wrought iron, and sculpture. He has often persuaded clients to retain interior details that they wanted to remove. Having done a majority of his work in Society Hill, Mark already had his architectural office and studio in a house he owns in the next street, before he bought this house directly behind it in 1969. He designed an apartment for himself on the ground floor, with a delightful garden created in the former baker's oven (*color, page 174*). His kitchen features a salvaged door with stained-glass insets, and a rough, stone vaulted ceiling (*141*). In his living room, he has exposed the structural stonework of the walls and beams, and added a Gaudìesque column (*143*). The kitchen of the rental duplex apartment upstairs has a stained glass window and a vintage stove (*color, page 173*).

Barn, Litchfield County, Connecticut

Bakery, Philadelphia, Pennsylvania

175

Barn, Litchfield County, Connecticut

Although the lovely property he bought in Litchfield County, Connecticut, included a handsome clapboard house, actor Michael Wager chose to restore and convert this 1820 dairy barn into a weekend home. He preferred the barn's wide-open space and rustic atmosphere as a setting for his elegant, eclectic furnishings. The building had a slanting floor, gaps in the siding, no heat, plumbing, or electricity, and the unusual square silo tilted away from the barn at a forty-five-degree angle. Nevertheless, Wager camped out in it for six months so that he could make decisions as work progressed, because he preferred to improvise his renovation rather than plan it in advance.

To retain the character of the barn and avoid rebuilding, he had polyurethane foam sprayed on all the interior walls. This effectively reinforced the 150-year-old siding, filling the gaps, as well as providing insulation. The exterior appearance is not changed at all (144), and on the interior, the foam molds itself to the contours of the rough-hewn lumber, so that it looks much as it did originally (color, page 176). The amber foam was painted white to contrast with the natural wood beams.

Slanting floors were straightened by cutting them into stepped levels. The large Palladian window, added to the side wall, was found in a junkyard for fifteen dollars. The leaning silo was jacked up and bolted onto the building. Inside, a handsome wooden spiral stairway leads up to Wager's bedroom, which has panoramic views of the rolling countryside. The entrance to Wager's silo suite is through a hinged section of the bookcase behind the piano. There are two more bedrooms off the other end of the living room: a charming little blue one (color, page 175), and another on a balcony over the kitchen. The ground floor has still more living-room space, plus another bedroom and bath at the bottom of the silo.

Coach House, Boston, Massachusetts

Built in 1895 as a coach house and stable for a Beacon Hill town house, this building (*145*) later became a firehouse when engines were still drawn by horses. It was then used as a warehouse until 1966, when a developer bought it and the two adjoining coach houses, for conversion to three town houses. Architects Marvin and Joan Goody (who live in a nearby converted coach house of their own) created the imaginative interiors. Their design around a glass-walled atrium overcomes the building's intrinsic problem—having no rear yard and only small windows opening onto the street. A potentially dark and gloomy interior has become a light-filled garden, achieving openness with privacy. This plan proved so successful that it set the style for other coach-house conversions in the block.

Each of the three town-house owners has adapted his atrium-centered home in a totally different style. The owners of this one enjoy the surprise of first-time guests as the feeling of the city disappears the moment they enter the door. The family finds its serenity tremendously appealing—though decorating and housekeeping present a challenge when almost all rooms are constantly in view.

The garden (*146*), which becomes an integral part of the decor, stays green year-round, except for the dogwood tree, whose bare branches take on a sculptural quality in winter. At Christmastime, a twelve-foot tree is placed in the pool, where it stands until spring, and its lights, diffused through an occasional snowfall, provide a lovely tableau for the city dwellers who have made their home in a stable.

146

147

Toy Factory, New York, New York

The twenty-six-block area called SoHo (for south of Houston Street) in lower Manhattan probably contains the greatest number of factory buildings adapted as living space, as well as the largest concentration of cast-iron architecture remaining anywhere. After a near brush with extinction by a planned expressway, SoHo was designated an historic district in 1973 in recognition of its importance as a repository of this nineteenth-century architectural form, regarded as the precursor of the skyscraper. This was the first system of prefabricated building. Its columns and arches, designed to imitate stone carving, could be ordered in parts from catalogues for on-site assembly, where they were bolted to building façades, the bolts hidden with rosettes, acanthus leaves, and other cast-iron decoration. There are important cast-iron buildings east of SoHo also, some in a shocking

state of neglect, and five significant early buildings by James Bogardus that were disassembled and catalogued in 1971 for future resurrection were stolen for sale as scrap metal.

SoHo has had a fascinating history. The area itself was recycled at least four times, as it was repeatedly transformed for totally different uses. It was America's first settlement of free blacks, when the Dutch West India Company liberated a group of slaves in 1644. The area in which they settled, north of the town of Nieuw Amsterdam, was rural farmland for more than a century, when it was leveled to become a prosperous residential district. By 1825, it was the city's finest neighborhood, lined with Federal brick town houses, of which some thirty still survive, sadly mutilated.

By the 1850s, the residential neighborhood was pushed northward, as large stores moved in

(in the first of a series of similar progressions up Manhattan island, as the business district moved to Fourteenth Street, then Twenty-third, Thirty-fourth, and on into the Forties and Fifties, always pushing the residential section ahead of it). Lord and Taylor, Tiffany & Co., and Brooks Brothers were among those that built stores (many of them cast-iron) in this area. Hotels, theaters, music halls, and a red-light district soon followed. Between 1860 and 1865 the area lost a quarter of its population through fear of the neighborhood, as Houston Street became "murderer's row."

Next came manufacturers, with their factories and warehouses. Many more elaborate cast-iron buildings were added to the stores that had been erected in the 1850s. Manufacturing and the construction of cast-iron buildings reached a peak in the 1870s, dwindled in the

1880s and 1890s, and died in the twentieth century. Although there was still commercial activity, many buildings were vacant, dingy, and neglected. In the 1960s, artists driven out of Greenwich Village by high prices discovered the huge, cheap spaces, ideal for their work. They began living there surreptitiously, because building department regulations made loft-living illegal. By 1971, the more than five hundred artists already in residence succeeded in persuading the city to bend the rules and legalize their occupancy—to the regret of many today, because SoHo became a victim of its own success. Galleries, followed by boutiques and restaurants, attracted weekend crowds. Doctors and lawyers have moved in among the artists (though the city waived the rules for artists only) as SoHo became chic, and the inevitable effect has been skyrocketing prices, which are bound

to drive out many of the artists again.

Hanford Yang, who lived in a house in Yonkers and rented office space on Twenty-third Street, bought a SoHo factory (147) to eliminate the time and expense of commuting as well as to satisfy his desire to own a cast-iron building. An architect who designs contemporary buildings, he had tremendous admiration and respect for the importance of this form as an influence on the development of today's architecture. Having read articles about SoHo, and knowing artists who lived there, he set out to find a building in late 1972, just before the area was designated an historic district. By then, prices had risen considerably (they are now approximately four times as high as they were ten years ago), so Mr. Yang found three other people, through advertising, who were willing to join him in purchasing cooperatively.

The building was a toy factory (erected in the 1870s), with the ground floor used as warehouse space, the second as offices, and the remainder, manufacturing. Though a firm was still in operation when he bought the building, they were planning a move to Queens for greater and lower-cost space. Mr. Yang took over the second floor as his office, the third as his home, and his partners in the cooperative each have one of the remaining floors above. The ground floor is rented out by the cooperative to the Visual Art Center of SoHo. The owners shared the cost of replacing the leaky roof, new heating, plumbing and wiring, and the major expense of a passenger elevator to replace the old freight elevator. The exterior of the building was painted with a color suggested by the Landmarks Commission, based on colors of the natural stone that cast iron was intended to imitate.

More recently, the blank side wall was decorated with a beautifully executed *trompe-l'oeil* mural *(150)* that repeats the façade motif (complete with air conditioners and a cat on a window sill). The painting was done by artist Richard Haas through City Walls, Inc., a nonprofit organization working with artists, landlords, and the community for improvement of the visual environment.

The cooperative members designed their own floors independently. Mr. Yang's is an open plan, with a minimum of walls; spaces are delineated by five different levels *(148, 149)*. At an angle across the rear, his bedroom and bath occupy the highest level, flowing down into the kitchen-dining level, surrounded by a low wall overlooking the large, open living room, which extends to the front windows of the building. Two more levels rise in this lowest space: a circular, or hexagonal, seating area, and along one wall, a horizontal line of cabinets with a built-in desk on a continuous platform. Utilities are concealed below the levels, and the entire surface is covered with gray carpeting. The openness, white walls and gray floors, broken only by the building's cast-iron columns, provides an ideal setting for Hanford Yang's fine collection of contemporary art. A Frank Lloyd Wright window, suspended from the ceiling, floats in the air several feet in front of the vertical blinds on the window wall.

The only drawback to Mr. Yang's pleasure in his cast-iron abode is the outrageous increase in real-estate taxes, from $600 to $2,700 per floor per year in the three years since the cooperative bought the building. This regressive nation-wide taxation policy rewards property owners for allowing buildings to disintegrate, while penalizing those who improve them. It is small wonder that our cities are in such a sorry state.

Otherwise, Hanford Yang is delighted with living in his former toy factory in SoHo. He finds the neighborhood safe, quiet (quieter than the wilderness on weekends), convenient, and exciting. The mixture of professional types who live there enjoy a mutual sense of brotherhood, respect, and protection. A quotation from Mr. Yang, designer of new buildings and teacher of contemporary architecture, sums up the philosophy of this book: "It takes many good buildings to form one good street, many good streets to form one good neighborhood, many good neighborhoods to form one good city. If a city has culture, certainly the buildings reflect it. No culture can be established overnight. No city should be designed and built all at once. To destroy good buildings without hesitation is really to destroy the culture of a city."

150

Firehouse, San Francisco, California

This San Francisco firehouse (152) had been decommissioned by the city and boarded up for about a year. Designer John Dickinson wanted to buy it, but was told it had been condemned, and would be auctioned off for the lot value. Since he was not interested in the lot, he went off on a trip to England, and forgot about it. Returning in 1963, he found that the real-estate speculator who had bought it was willing to sell it to him.

The building had been maintained in excellent condition by carpenters who carefully copied details when they made repairs. The only structural change necessary was in the creation of a dressing room and kitchen. Though the bathroom had two showers and six or seven wash basins, the size was left the same when the fixtures were removed. All other changes were cosmetic (151; color, page 185). Dickinson is pleased with how well the building works as his home and office—his stationery is crested with an embossed fire hose, like the one coiled around the date on the front of his building.

151

Cotton Warehouse, Savannah, Georgia

Cotton Warehouse, Savannah, Georgia

Savannah was built on a century of prosperity in the cotton trade through its port on the Savannah River. It was here that the artist who researched Savannah's early colors found a 150-year-old cotton warehouse on the waterfront and made it into a home.

Though the building was in filthy condition, Ann Osteen fell in love with its tremendous space, and the patchwork-quilt effect of its stone walls. The oldest cotton warehouse in Georgia, it was built in 1814–18 with ships' ballast from all over the world—semi-precious stones, lava, fool's gold, sea shells, fossils, Mediterranean coral, chunks of coal (153). The first steamship to cross the Atlantic, the *Savannah,* left from the William Taylor wharf on which the warehouse is built.

Factor's Walk, the row of river-front warehouses, with their picturesque ramps and

153

bridged walkways, had already become offices on the city side, but the river side was a derelict assortment of strip joints and bars when Dr. and Mrs. Osteen decided to make their home there. Banks, usually reluctant to finance such a project, had learned from the successful restoration of Savannah, and a mortgage was provided in order to help open up the river front. It worked; a total metamorphosis within two years, that made this a highly desirable location for boutiques and restaurants. Now there are government plans to exploit the waterfront with a sunken amphitheatre, yacht harbor, and boatels.

Raised to appreciate antiques by a mother who was an authority, Ann Osteen wanted to use the best that remained in the old building

while creating beautiful contemporary loft-style open space. She parted company from the first two architects she spoke to, because they wanted to throw out the immense wheel that served as a hoist for cotton bales. She has it hung horizontally from the rafters like a great sculpture (154). Open stairways, skylights, and soaring spaces, curved walls, strong colors, and doors swinging on a single, central pivot make a dramatic contemporary environment, softened by weathered beams, old stone walls, and an eclectic collection of furniture (color, page 186). Through a trap door in the floor, Ann Osteen can descend to a huge painting studio. Below her studio, on the river side, where the building has an additional floor, is space that is rented out to two craft shops.

Dr. and Mrs. Osteen could have lived in any city, but chose Savannah because of its marvelous old buildings and restoration activity, in which she soon became involved after arriving in the early 1960s. She was asked to do a visual survey of lights and signs, but her outstanding contribution to the Historic Savannah Foundation was in researching the early Savannah colors. She worked out a strong, vibrant spectrum, based on scraping back layers of old paint, and her findings were confirmed by the portfolio of a nineteenth-century Savannah muralist. The colors are now produced commercially under names taken from Savannah folklore. The first she found was christened Haint Blue—the color that the blacks used to paint windows and doors to keep out the evil spirits.

Church, Glenelg, Maryland

Occasionally someone drives up to this charming little white church *(155)* set on a knoll at a rural Maryland crossroads, to ask when the services are held. But inside the arched doorway a strikingly spacious, contemporary home has been created by architect William Potts for his family *(156)*. Mr. and Mrs. Potts chose to make their home in Providence Church not only because they found it appealing, but because they would have the space they needed for half the cost of a comparable new building. Tatiana Potts has a professional pottery workshop, William Potts has an office, each of their three children has a bedroom, and there is even a children's living room behind the stairway where the altar used to be. Mrs. Potts, formerly a concert cellist, is enthusiastic about the fine acoustics the church provides for her chamber music group.

She is also intrigued by the Civil War history of the area—Harpers Ferry is nearby. This is a borderline area that is very Southern, so there were two Methodist churches, built a half-mile apart. Providence Church, built in 1889, was the Southern Methodist church. The two were merged in 1962, and this one, the smaller, was abandoned. When the Potts family found it, many of the windows were broken, the paint was peeling, there was no plumbing and minimal electricity. Within nine months they accomplished this lovely example of restoration and adaptive use. Virtually all of the original elements of the church were retained and restored. Stained glass windows were repaired, matching original color and texture, and two of the pews provide seating at the dining table.

Schoolhouse, Charlestown, Massachusetts

Charlestown, on a hilly peninsula across the Charles River from Boston, predates Boston by one year. Founded in 1629, it was burned by the British in 1775 in the Battle of Bunker Hill. It was rebuilt in the period after the Revolution, and at the turn of the century was one of Boston's most elegant neighborhoods, with a population of sixty thousand. Construction of an elevated railway on Main Street drove out aristocratic families, and the population dropped to twelve thousand. Homes were taken over by the mid-nineteenth-century influx of Irish immigrants, and Charlestown remained a close-knit, stable community.

Charlestown's variety of Federal, Greek revival, Mansard, and bracketed house styles are attracting more and more Bostonians as homeowners. However, Peter Staaterman, who had already tried his hand at renovation of a house for investment in Boston's South End, turned his attention to a different sort of building for his own home in Charlestown. Staaterman had heard that the old schoolhouse facing Winthrop Square would be put up for sale, and he went to have a look at it. The square was the old militia training field prior to the British conflagration. It is said that the school was built in the center of it in 1826. Some twenty years later, the two-story school was moved to the edge of the square, where it was raised up and placed on a new ground floor to become a three-story building—which accounts for its strangely vertical proportions. It was used by the city as a public school until it was sold to the Roman Catholic archdiocese for a parochial school, remaining in use until 1972.

Peter Staaterman found its brick façade painted an ugly pink beige, its rooms lined with desks screwed to the floors, blackboards on the walls, and statuettes of the Virgin Mary adorning the corners. There were large soapstone sinks on each floor, pull-chain toilets, acoustical tile ceilings, and fluorescent strip lighting. The windows, placed high off the floors, provided no view of the square for the students. In spite of this unappealing interior, Staaterman was attracted by the potential provided by the large open space. Climbing up a ladder attached to the wall, he knew he wanted the building when he saw the structural beams supporting the roof; those beams have become a major decorative feature of Staaterman's apartment.

He called in architect Calvin Opitz, with whom he had worked on his South End house, to design his spacious apartment (158) and four rental units. The exterior brick (157) and interior woodwork were stripped of paint. The handsome walls and beams were exposed, and the window-height problem was solved by building up the floors to form multilevel interiors. The old schoolhouse on the lovely, historic square, has been reborn as a spacious, attractive dwelling.

157

Bottling Plant:
Offices, Brooklyn, New York

In the heart of Brooklyn's Bedford-Stuyvesant district, an abandoned milk-bottling plant, symbol of the decay infecting this black ghetto, has been transformed into a contemporary six-story office building (159), headquarters of the Bedford-Stuyvesant Restoration Corporation. Designed by a black architect and carried out by a black contracting team recruited from the community, this project epitomizes the imaginative program conceived by Robert F. Kennedy for the total physical, economic, and social rehabilitation of a 657-square-block area of over four-hundred thousand people, an entire "city" stricken with severe urban blight and despair. Since the area has many fine nineteenth-century buildings (including a designated historic district) and it has been proven psychologically beneficial to retain a familiar environment, the philosophy of the program is to restore rather than demolish, wherever possible.

This building (160, 161) includes ground-floor offices for a bank, utility, and telephone company, and a beautifully equipped theater for black cultural performances. An ice-skating rink, built directly behind it, will be surrounded by a shopping complex created through a combination of new construction and renovation of forgotten factory buildings, tied together with malls, arcades, and plazas. The complex provides a center for a sprawling community that has never had a focal point.

160

159

Factories: **Ghirardelli Square, San Francisco, California**

Ghirardelli Square was a trend-setter. Its highly successful re-use of a group of old buildings inspired nationwide imitations, which continue to spring up everywhere in a multitude of variations.

Ghirardelli was an Italian who brought his business in chocolate and spices to San Francisco by way of South America. He arrived at the time of the 1849 gold rush, but it was not until 1892 that his sons bought the two-and-a-half-acre site on San Francisco Bay to carry on their father's thriving business. Their purchase included the Woolen Mill (165), one of the West's oldest factories, where Civil War uniforms were manufactured. Between 1900 and 1916, the Ghirardellis built a group of crenellated brick buildings around the old mill, to house their chocolate and spice business. Their huge Ghirardelli sign became a San Francisco landmark, visible to every ship entering the harbor until it went dark during World War II.

In 1962, when the business was sold and moved to San Leandro, a group headed by William Roth bought the property to prevent its loss to new high-rise construction and to retain the important open space on the bay opposite Fisherman's Wharf. Architects, landscape archi-

Factories: **Ghirardelli Square,
San Francisco, California**

166

167

tects, and designers were employed to restore and adapt the old factory buildings to a complex of shops, restaurants, and theaters. Views from the exceptionally beautiful site have been skillfully exploited, and the weaving together of multilevel interiors around delightful open spaces provides exciting variety in the Ghirardelli Square experience (162, 163). The character of the original architecture, particularly the old clock tower (164), modeled after the Blois chateau in France, contributes its special charm, and the careful screening of tenants, plus control of design and graphics, add to the total effectiveness of the complex.

Ghirardelli Square opened in 1964; and though the complex was not entirely completed until 1968, it soon began winning awards and widespread fame. It became a prime attraction, and hordes of visitors came to admire it and mispronounce its name (Gear-ar-delly).

One of its earliest imitators was the Cannery, just across the street. The Cannery (166, 167) was conceived while neighboring Ghirardelli Square was under construction, when Leonard Martin purchased the old Del Monte canning factory on San Francisco Bay. The building (ca. 1894) predates the 1906 earthquake, and all of the Ghirardelli structures except the Woolen Mill. Martin's idea was to save it from the wrecker's ball, and transform it into a festive bazaar with the flavor of a European marketplace. Commissioning a fine architect, designer, and landscape artist, and sparing nothing in taste, care, or money, he produced a highly successful, award-winning, people-oriented environment for shopping, dining, and entertainment. The old brick exterior of the factory was restored to enclose a three-level walled city, its interior redesigned into a maze of alleys, arcades, bridges, balconies, ramps, and stairways that invite exploration and

discovery. A dramatic, open elevator in the interior courtyard contributes to the concept of using the movement of people as an integral element of the building's visual impact. The courtyard was planned as a social center, where the public is encouraged to sit under the eighty-year-old olive trees and enjoy performances of chamber music, mime, magic, singers, and street musicians. The Cannery's emblem is adapted from the design of the tie-rod bolts that reinforced the old factory walls. The new interior structure is enriched by ancient treasures that Martin bought from the William Randolph Hearst estate; a thirteenth-century Byzantine ceiling ornaments a clothing store, and seventeenth-century English oak paneling, carved mantels, and a Jacobean staircase designed by Inigo Jones are installed in the hundred-foot-long hall of the Ben Jonson pub, one of The Cannery's wide variety of restaurants.

Theater: **Opera House, East Haddam, Connecticut**

Quiet little East Haddam was a popular summer resort when William Goodspeed built his dramatic opera house high on the bank of the Connecticut River, its rear landing designed to receive disembarking steamboat and ferry passengers. River steamers were then the chief mode of travel; there was daily service in each direction between New York and Hartford (an overnight trip) with a stop at East Haddam en route.

Flamboyant William Goodspeed was a successful merchant, banker, shipbuilder, hotel owner, and steamboat and railroad tycoon. He planned to serve all purposes with his opera house—people could arrive on his steamers, spend the night at his adjacent hotel, buy almost anything at his general store on the ground floor of the opera-house building, and enjoy fine entertainment in his beautiful theater on the top

two floors. It was the finest available entertainment; he was known to import entire shows from Broadway on his steamers, often just for one-night stands. People came from miles around in carriages, buggies, surreys, sleighs, and of course, steamer, ferry, and rowboat.

People are coming from miles around once more to enjoy the reincarnation of the Goodspeed Opera House (169), although it had been scheduled for extinction, and had a last-minute rescue almost as dramatic as the performances on its stage. The demolition order lay on the desk of the state highway commissioner when Mrs. Alfred Howe Terry of the Antiquarian Landmarks Society wrote begging him not to sign. The building had been used by Connecticut as a warehouse and garage for state highway trucks, from 1943 until after World War II, and since then, fallen into disuse, it stood empty

and forlorn. The state had decided to replace it with a concrete garage, when a citizen's committee was organized to save it. Support was solicited from Governor Abraham Ribicoff, and the state legislature subsequently agreed to weatherproof and maintain it for five years while the newly-formed Goodspeed Opera House Foundation raised funds for its restoration—both physically, and as a playhouse.

Within a year, restoration was under way, inaugurated by a plaster-ripping party, in which hundreds took part, including legislators, bankers, lawyers, and the governor. The result is part restoration, part adaptive use. The stage and horseshoe-shaped balcony, with its gold-leaf rococo decoration, have been beautifully restored (168): even the original drop curtain, painted with a steamboat, has been retrieved and rehung. The steamer, *State of New York,* had

169

170

been painted on the curtain to create the illusion that the audience was looking through the building to the river itself. Ironically, the *State of New York* later sank just behind the opera house, near the point at which it is depicted on the curtain.

The floors below the theater (nineteenth-century theaters made their audiences climb several flights of stairs to the auditorium), which formerly housed Goodspeed's offices and general store, have been converted to an elegant bar and refreshment rooms, lobby, and box offices. The center of the lobby features a splendid staircase designed in the steamboat tradition *(170).*

The theater reopened in 1963, and in 1965, *Man of La Mancha* was born there. Innovative artistic director Michael Price plans to dedicate the Goodspeed Opera House to the best of American musical theater, past and future. A recent success was the first professional production of John Philip Sousa's *El Capitan* since its debut in 1896.

The theater's successful restoration has revived East Haddam. Houses are being restored as homes, and for new businesses, which indicate proximity to the Goodspeed Opera House in their advertising; once more proving that restoration can be good for business.

Michael Price has also been instrumental in forming the League of Historic American Theaters. There are many vintage theaters being revived and restored: among them the Central City, Tabor, and Wheeler opera houses in Central City, Leadville, and Aspen, Colorado; the Springer Opera House in Columbus, Georgia; and the Promised Valley Playhouse in Salt Lake City, Utah.

Railway Car: **Restaurant, Aspen, Colorado**

Built in 1887 as a luxurious private railway car *(171)*, and used for hunting trips by Theodore Roosevelt, this rare relic of a bygone era was found on a Colorado ranch, where it was serving as a chicken coop. The roof was off, and the interior had been painted white by a family that lived in it during the Depression. Though he had no idea what he would do with it, Tim Terral bought it and moved it to Aspen, where he began a long, careful restoration. He stripped the paint off the Honduras mahogany walls and restored the ceiling with its fleur-de-lis motif, authenticated through research at the Chicago Railway Museum. The original lighting fixtures, found hanging from the broken roof, were restored and replaced.

As a setting for his handsomely refurbished coach, Terral rebuilt a section of track on the old Colorado-Midland right of way, on which the parlor car used to run. There it began a new life as a gourmet restaurant, with four private dining rooms. From the observation platform, diners enter the parlor to wait on red, plush Victorian furniture to be shown to a table in one of the compartments *(color, page 203)*, which were originally bedroom, study, dining room, and porter's room. The elegant atmosphere is enhanced by candlelight. Terral claims there are ghosts (happy ghosts)—and perhaps they contribute to the almost tangible aura that pervades the Parlour Car Restaurant. The restaurant is open at night during the skiing season, when the hillside is always shrouded with snow, illuminated solely by the lights from the parlor car. The theatrical effect prepares the visitor for the illusion of stepping back into the nineteenth century.

171

Movie Theater: **Symphony Hall, St. Louis, Missouri**

In recent years, as television made them obsolete, the enormous, ornate palaces built in the 1920s and 1930s for movies and vaudeville have been scorned as ridiculous and impractical. Considered as expendable as Victorian houses, they joined the list of candidates for demolition, becoming another endangered species of our not-so-distant past. Soon our children might have no opportunity to see the mammoth splendor of these monuments to the silver screen.

The St. Louis Theater was built in 1926 on Grand Avenue, the Broadway of St. Louis, where it was one of six theaters in five blocks. The opening stage show featured Singer's midgets, elephants, ponies, and dogs. By the 1960s, television had taken its toll of motion-picture theaters, and there were no more stage shows between films. The company that owned the St. Louis also owned the gigantic Fox Theater across the street, which was more than ample to accommodate movie-goers. These two were the last remaining Grand Avenue theaters; the neighborhood was in decline and the demise of the St. Louis Theater could endanger their investment in the Fox. The last picture show exhibited within its dingy, peeling walls was, prophetically, *The Sound of Music*.

In 1966, the St. Louis Symphony decided to adopt this abandoned movie palace as its first permanent home. The second oldest symphony orchestra in America (founded in 1880), it had never had a home of its own. For years the orchestra performed in the vast Kiel Opera House, where enthusiastic audiences at adjacent, simultaneous sporting events often drowned out the music. On one occasion, a boisterous party in another part of the multipurpose hall caused light bulbs to fall into the string section.

A $500,000 gift with an approaching deadline gave the Symphony's search for a home a pressing urgency. Knowing that a new hall would cost $15 million to $20 million, and that many recently built at astronomical cost suffered acoustical problems, the Symphony Society decided to consider adaptive use of an existing building. Their need fortuitously coincided with the availability of the old movie theater. The Symphony had once played a special concert there, and the acoustics had proved surprisingly good. Tests by experts determined that the old St. Louis Theater should begin a glorious new life as Powell Symphony Hall (named for the donor of an initial $1 million gift). A successful fund-raising drive was launched and architects, acoustics and lighting experts, designers, and contractors were brought in. Worn terazzo in the spectacular lobby was covered with marble, chandeliers were rehung with Italian crystal, stairs and halls covered with red carpet, walls and ceiling painted cream white *(color, page 204)*. So much gold leaf was required to gild the plaster decoration that the American supply was exhausted, and more had to be flown in from Germany. The concrete auditorium floor was covered with a double layer of wood for resonance, the eight-story stage lowered to a five-story permanent shell, and walls and doors sound-proofed to insure that only music would be heard inside the hall *(172)*.

A sadly ironic touch: the bar of the late New York Metropolitan Opera House adorns the lobby. Poor New York City no longer has a concert hall that equals the splendor of this one, with the elegant surroundings that enhance audience enjoyment and sense of occasion.

The completely renovated old movie theater proved a success. Not only was it praised for its beauty and fine acoustics, but it has made a tremendous difference to the well-being of the St. Louis Symphony. After playing to empty seats in a hall with poor acoustics, they were virtually sold out by the time they had been in their new home for two years, with attendance more than doubled. For a change, the musicians could hear themselves and each other. The grandeur of their environment gave them a feeling they were appreciated, resulting in a new *esprit de corps*.

There is no question that the Symphony saved at least $10 million by adapting this building instead of constructing a new one, nor is there any doubt of its beneficial effect on the neighborhood. However, the greatest proof of success is imitation. The conversion of the St. Louis Theater to Powell Symphony Hall was soon followed by the adaptation of a Pantages movie house in Pittsburgh to the Heinz Hall for the Performing Arts, a Warner Brothers Cinema to the Youngstown Symphony Center in Ohio. More recently, the art deco Paramount Theater in Oakland, California, was bought by the Oakland Symphony and restored as a music and dance center.

172

A unique example of adaptive use is the conversion of the Crown Hill Cemetery waiting station to headquarters of the Historic Landmarks Foundation of Indiana. This handsome little brick building *(173)* with its intricate terra-cotta decoration, is a fine example of high Victorian Gothic style, and has been maintained in excellent condition since it was built in 1885. Its original purpose was to shelter people arriving for funerals until the assembled mourners could proceed to the chapel. Crown Hill is a large, beautiful, and famous cemetery, boasting the graves of such disparate celebrities as John Dillinger and James Whitcomb Riley.

A new chapel and modern transportation facilities made the waiting station obsolete, and since it was too small for the cemetery's administration offices, the Historic Landmarks Foundation of Indiana decided to adapt it for their use in 1971. Relatively few changes were necessary, other than central air conditioning and a few other modernizations. The handsome woodwork is said to have come from trees on the grounds; the huge chandelier is from a building in Philadelphia *(174)*.

176

The transformation of Baltimore's Mt. Royal Station into an art school is a multifaceted success story. The Maryland Institute College of Art, second oldest art school in America, celebrates its 150th birthday in 1976, but for a while its chances for survival seemed bleak. In 1961, when Eugene W. Leake took over as president, it was a dying institution, with an enrollment that had dwindled to three hundred. Today the student body is up to 1,500; the staff, faculty, and salaries have multiplied; and an endowment that started at zero has grown through contributions to $100,000 a year.

By a happy combination of circumstances, the school's need for expansion coincided with the railroad station's abandonment. Maryland Institute's original home is a handsome 1907 building located in Bolton Hill, Baltimore's most successful restoration neighborhood, within sight of Mt. Royal Station. The school first acquired additional space in a nearby row house, and later went on to occupy a total of nine buildings; all but the first were recycled.

Built in 1899 in a grassy bowl surrounded by park land, the Renaissance railroad station, with its 150-foot clock tower, became a favorite Baltimore landmark *(177)*. Its grand, colonnaded interior *(176)* held nostalgic memories of wedding trips, soldiers going off to war, and family reunions, as well as visits of Woodrow Wilson, Herbert Hoover, Calvin Coolidge, Franklin D. Roosevelt, Dwight D. Eisenhower, and even Buffalo Bill. Arturo Toscanini dined in a private car at Mt. Royal before appearing at the Lyric Theater across the street. No one in Baltimore wanted to see it go. But in 1961 the Baltimore and Ohio, having canceled passenger service from Washington to New York, was forced to close it

down. The Maryland Institute's need came just in time to save the building from vandals.

The school actually had a tryout period in the station while the railroad company searched for a suitable purchaser. The experiment worked so well that the school decided they must either find a way to buy the building or move out of the city. The Baltimore and Ohio finally made it possible by selling them the station plus several acres of land for $250,000, in effect, a substantial contribution. It was still a tremendous gamble, because the school had no money for the renovation. Six-hundred thousand dollars was borrowed against pledges of contributions, and eventually the drive exceeded $1 million.

A major goal in the conversion was to retain every feature of the original building. Additional floor space was gained with a second floor at the balcony level, glassing-in the arches around an open court in the center *(175)*. The second floor is now a spacious library. One side of the ground floor is a lecture hall, the other a gallery, both with movable walls. Enclosing the baggage and waiting platforms provided space for sculpture studios, photography gallery, and cafeteria. Third-floor lofts have been transformed into painting studios. Construction costs came to eighteen dollars per square foot as opposed to twenty-five dollars per square foot for new construction.

The result is an unqualified success. The students have a great affection for the building, and because people loved it as a landmark, new interest has been attracted to the school. Fund raising has become easier, and substantial contributions were made toward the renovation (one family gave $250,000). The architect and contractor have won many awards for their work.

177

House: **Hotel, Galena, Illinois**

Strange as it may seem, Galena was once far more prosperous than Chicago, and in 1845, when it claimed to be the world's foremost lead-mining town, it was the largest river port north of St. Louis. Like Ste. Genevieve, Galena's fortune was based on lead and the Mississippi River. During the town's peak years, Ulysses S. Grant lived in Galena (as well as in Covington, Kentucky); when he returned in glory from the war in 1865, the citizens were so proud that they built a house for him (now a museum). But the Fever River, Galena's four-mile tributary to the Mississippi, silted up, the demand for lead dropped off, and railroads replaced river transport.

Just like other towns that went to sleep for

several decades, Galena emerged unchanged into the twentieth century. Nineteenth-century mansions are handsomely set off by the exceptional topography—steep, wooded hills (with flights of steps from the main street) surrounding a river valley. The citizens, aware of their town's special quality, show their well-preserved houses on an annual house tour. A number have become museums, and the few that were in bad shape have been restored.

The Belvedere, shown here, symbolizes the quixotic fate of Galena. This majestic 1857 Victorian mansion, with its bracketed cupola (178), was set high on the bank of the river by its builder, steamship owner J. Russell Jones. Jones must have had a fine vantage point for survey-

179

ing his steamboat empire from this luxurious villa, said to have been decades ahead of its time, with three systems of running water: hot, cold, and iced. Today it is hard to believe that this shrunken rivulet ever carried steamboats, or came near the door of the Belvedere. Jones was appointed ambassador to Belgium by his friend, President Grant, and never returned. Everyone who owned the house after him seems to have suffered misfortune.

The house is said to be haunted by the ghost of a nine-year-old boy named Lester, a child who suffocated when he climbed into a coffin in the attic in the 1890s. Now he goes about opening closed doors. Successive owners lost fortunes, or were involved in other bizarre deaths. More than once the house was sold for back taxes, and finally stood empty, open to anyone who cared to wander in. In 1961, it was rescued from impending ruin and restored as a hotel, with beautifully decorated bedrooms full of antique furniture. People drove 160 miles from Chicago just for the pleasure of staying there for the weekend. But the jinx struck again. The new owner, who arrived with a $150,000 inheritance, left $200,000 in debt, after being cheated by a partner. Bankruptcy proceedings, too large to be accommodated in Galena, had to be held in neighboring Freeport in two day-long sessions. Luckily, the judge had a fondness for the Belvedere, and rather than selling it off piece-by-piece, allowed what was left to be purchased intact.

An elderly restaurateur bought it for a nephew who rejected it. The new owner has added antique furnishings to those that remained in the handsome bedrooms, striving to resurrect the former splendor (179). Adaptations of homes to inns are, of course, quite common and not at all new. The 1845 Jared Coffin House in Nantucket, Massachusetts, became a hotel in 1847.

Library: **Theater, New York, New York**

Bought by a developer for demolition in 1965, the Astor Library was the first building to be saved under the New York Landmarks Preservation Act. It was built as a palatial setting for John Jacob Astor's private library; begun in 1849, the original building was expanded twice, with work on the third section continuing into the 1880s. It was later given to the city as the first free Public Library. When the collection was combined with the Tilden and Lenox libraries, the Public Library was moved uptown to its new home on Fifth Avenue and Forty-second Street. This monument to private wealth then became the Hebrew Immigrant Aid Society, its magnificent soaring halls rimmed with colonnaded balconies partitioned into cubicles to provide temporary shelter for the homeless.

At the time that the Hebrew Immigrant Aid Society was seeking a purchaser for the build-

ing, the New York Shakespeare Festival was looking for a permanent home, but its dismal appearance caused associate producer Bernard Gersten to reject it when he first saw it. Until that time, Joseph Papp's Shakespeare Festival had produced three plays performed without admission charge each summer in an outdoor theater in Central Park, with only occasional winter productions. Plans for year-round performances, including new plays, required a building to house theater and offices. New construction was being considered when the newly formed Landmarks Commission designated the Astor Library a landmark, won a six-month reprieve from demolition, and called Papp, asking him to look at it again. This time Papp, Gersten, and scene designer Ming Cho Lee looked at it and liked it.

Papp and architect Giorgio Cavaglieri worked

together to create three theaters, offices, and rehearsal halls within the handsome interior, without destroying its character *(180)*. Cavaglieri ruefully points out things that were never completed for lack of funds, but when money is available, theater production always takes precedence. At one point, impending financial disaster was averted when Papp persuaded the city to buy the building and lease it back to the company for one dollar a year.

The first production in the renovated building was the fantastically successful *Hair*, followed by three award-winning plays, all of which moved on to Broadway. Papp is now also director of the Lincoln Center Theater, but he prefers to spend his time working in the converted Astor Library building *(181)*, which he no longer thinks of as a landmark building, but as a permanent home.

182

Houses: **Dormitories, Offices, and Apartments, Charleston, South Carolina**

Rather than destroy old buildings for expansion of their facilities, the College of Charleston acquired sixty houses adjacent to their central campus for adaptive use: three are eighteenth-century, three-quarters are nineteenth-century, and all were built as homes. They have been adapted as contemporary offices, classrooms, and dormitories. (183). A master plan coordinates preservation and construction programs in terms of building proportions, materials, colors, landscapes and streetscapes. Here is a truly commendable, sensitively executed example of responsible recycling.

The Palladian villa shown here (182) was built in 1832 with the finest materials available —mahogany stairway, marble mantels, silver door knobs—as one of Charleston's great mansions. Occupied by Union troops after the fall of Charleston in the Civil War, it was converted to a negro hotel by the Northern conquerors. Following failure of the hotel, it was a home once more until the 1930s, when it was divided into six apartments. During World War II, the area began to disintegrate, and the house along with it. The mansion seemed doomed in 1964, when the Charleston Housing Authority planned a low-rent housing project on the site, but the Historic Charleston Foundation purchased the building to save it. Making sufficient repairs to weatherproof the house, the Foundation held it until a purchaser could be found to restore it to a useful life. At last it was sold to the Arthur Ravenel, Jr., Real Estate Company for their headquarters, with the top floors restored as three luxury apartments. There has been much adaptive use of this sort in Charleston, and the Historic Charleston Foundation has usually been instrumental in making it happen.

Warehouses: **Old Port Exchange, Portland, Maine**

An exciting transformation is taking place on Portland's waterfront *(184)*. Vacant, decaying, abandoned warehouse and commercial buildings are being adapted to new use as stores, restaurants, and offices, revitalizing a dead area and returning Portland's focal point to the waterfront, where it began. This is not government-sponsored urban renewal. It began in spite of municipal and banking indifference, through the vision and enterprise of individuals.

Portland's economic stability was established by its harbor, one of the best on the East Coast. Its prosperous exporting and shipbuilding industries all but ended after World War II, when the shipyards closed. Though it continues as an oil port, dry cargo handling has dwindled almost to a halt. By 1966, the whole area was virtually vacant.

Henry Willette is credited with being the first who saw the potential of the area and invested his money there. Willette, then with the city's planning department, was unable to convince the department or planning board of the area's potential. They felt that demolition, rather than redevelopment should be the approach to waterfront decay. Willette went ahead

on his own, purchasing a building in 1967, without the bank financing that he tried, and failed, to get. He refurbished empty shop fronts and rented to artisans and craftsmen. Some businesses failed, others succeeded. Meanwhile, other businessmen were attracted, particularly Frank Akers, who has since invested in a number of properties and gone into restoration on a large scale. Restaurants began opening, their success breeding success, attracting other businesses, and bringing evening traffic into the area.

At last the city and banks were convinced and joined in the revival. The city installed badly needed new street lighting, brick sidewalks, trees, and benches. When an investor could resell a $4,700 property a year later for $30,000, banks decided the Old Port Exchange was a good risk after all.

As it evolves into the city's new commercial center, the Old Port Exchange is becoming far more attractive than Portland's Commercial Street downtown. The value of the old architecture is being respected and played up, and signs are restrained and in good taste. No one is violating ground-floor façades with plate glass

and stainless steel, or attempting to attract customers with neon.

And it works. Joseph's men's clothing store had only been open two weeks when this picture was taken *(186)*, and the owners were astounded at how much business they had attracted already, with their low-key sign and exposed brick-and-beam interior.

The stairway shown here *(185)* spirals up the center of an old office building which had become a paper warehouse, then the home of a commune before it was leased and restored by Murray, Plumb and Murray, a law firm. Partner Peter Murray declares that he has gone from being a convert to an evangelist on the merits of working in the Old Port Exchange. Not only does he love working in the building, but he feels it has added to his firm's prestige, setting it apart as unique. Other lawyers who have seen its offices have contracted for space above Joseph's clothing store, which is being designed and built for them by architect Roger Ingalls, who owns the building. Ingalls is also including apartments in the building, which were in demand before they were finished.

185

186

House: **Newspaper Office, Savannah, Georgia**

187

188

The 1813 Oliver Sturges house *(188)*, one of the ten oldest houses remaining in Savannah, and considered one of the finest restorations in the city, is a notably successful adaptation—business offices and headquarters of the Morris Newspaper Corporation. Its twin house next door had long since been demolished and replaced by a hotel. The Sturges house, vacant since 1963, was saved from a similar fate by the Historic Savannah Foundation. Efforts to interest a church in using the building were fruitless, and neither could the C. & S. Bank, which owned it, be persuaded to turn it into a gentlemen's club. Historic Savannah could not afford to buy it, and the savings bank would give them a loan only if an individual put up collateral; attorney Walter Hartridge put up the deed on his own property to secure the loan. According to Mr. Hartridge, Historic Savannah was facing bankruptcy carrying this house and others that it was holding to resell for restoration. No wonder everyone in the city is grateful to Charles Morris, and proud of his beautiful restoration of this historic building.

Charles Morris came to Savannah when the Historic Savannah Foundation was in its infancy. A trustee of the organization, he credits the restoration movement with influencing his decision to make his headquarters in the city, though his company owns and operates newspapers in fifteen towns, and it would have been more convenient for him to locate elsewhere. When he left his father's newspaper organization to start his own, he decided to buy and restore an old building, rather than move into modern offices.

After buying the Sturges house, he employed architect Robert Gunn to put it back just as it was. Great pains were taken in repairing and replacing all original details *(187, 189)*, while unobtrusively concealing modern necessities. Gunn estimates that the cost was roughly comparable to a new building, but the advantages are clearly manifold. Charles Morris finds the building more functional than he thought it would be, and good for his company's reputation as well. Savannah appreciates it; though there was only a small notice in the paper, and it was a hot summer day, people drove in from miles around for the opening celebration. A couple of hundred were expected, but four thousand copies of a special magazine section about the house were given away to visitors, and people are still coming to see the house a year later.

190

Mill: **Architect's Office, Imlaystown, New Jersey**

Robert Zion, a landscape architect, feels that old buildings should be put back to work. In his view, a museum is somewhat dead and rather sad; for a building to be happy, it must be lived in and used. Since that is the philosophy of this book, Zion's conversion of Salter's Mill to the headquarters of Zion and Breen Associates is an apt example of adaptive re-use.

The original mill dates back to 1695, though it was rebuilt on the same foundations after an 1897 fire. One of its early millers, with Richard Salter, was Mordecai Lincoln, great-great-grandfather of Abraham Lincoln. After 265 years of grinding wheat, corn, oats, and barley, the old grist mill closed in 1962. In 1971, it was judged hazardous and condemned to be destroyed (190).

Robert Zion, who spent weekends on his nearby farm (where he lives in an old building), drove past the mill in the sleepy little village of Imlaystown, on his way back to work at his New York City office. When he learned it was doomed, he bought it to prevent its demolition, without having any idea what he would do with it. Finding it increasingly difficult to leave the

Denver, Colorado

country to return to work, he conceived the idea of moving his business to the mill. A number of Zion and Breen's employees already lived in New Jersey, and his partner was easily persuaded that a firm of landscape architects might indeed thrive in a country setting.

Zion modestly contends that the building (191) designed itself, that the spaces were already there, and he simply made the obvious use of them. However, saving all the mill parts and machinery and working them into the design of a handsome, functional, working office was an artful accomplishment, and beautifully executed.

Entering the front door, the visitor is greeted by the delightful sound of water running through the mill race. He is not yet inside the building proper, but standing on a slatted bridge, some 10 feet above the mill stones and running water, in a barnlike enclosure of rough-hewn old beams and rafters. Opposite, at the end of the bridge, is a red door in the stone wall of the building. Visible through large plate glass windows is the bright, contemporary reception area straight ahead (color, page 221), and an employees' lounge down below. It is a short walk from one era into another.

Everywhere throughout the four levels, clean modern lines and open spaces are interrupted with the bins, wheels, and pulleys of the mill machinery that Zion carefully preserved (192, 193). It has all been kept in working condition —the mill pulleys were used to hoist furniture to the upper floors. It is a stunning example of the combination of preservation and contemporary design.

Zion is able to ride his horse to work, and the firm has reduced its work week to four days. Though normally landscape architects are expected to meet with clients in the architect's office, an increasing number of their customers come to them, attracted by their delightful surroundings.

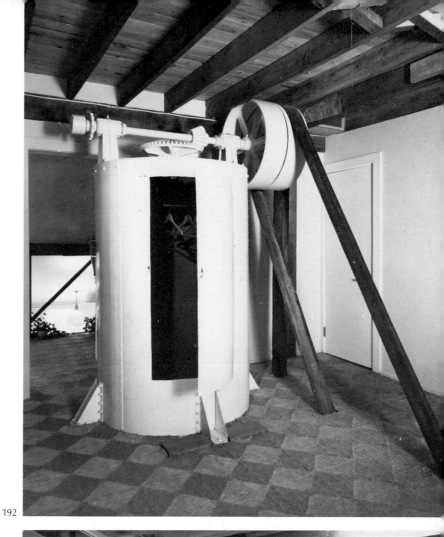

192

193

Skid Row: **Larimer Square, Denver, Colorado**

Larimer Square is not a square, but a block, lined on either side with Denver's oldest commercial buildings: almost the only old buildings left in the Skyline renewal area of downtown Denver. The city was founded on this site in 1858, and the 1400 block of Larimer Street included the city's first pharmacy, dry goods store, newspaper office, library, and bank. A hundred years later it was skid row—flophouses and saloons. This block probably would have been demolished also if it hadn't been for Dana and John Crawford.

The Crawfords were distressed at the sorry state of Denver's first main street and earliest buildings, so without any assurance that the area would be spared by urban renewal, they formed a corporation to buy, restore, renovate, and redesign the run-down Victorian buildings into a unified group of shops, galleries, offices, restaurants, and entertainment centers. Their concept was to "recapture the gay and boisterous spirit of Denver's youthful era."

Work began in 1965, and in 1974 Larimer Square got an unprecedented $2 million long-term loan from New York Life Insurance to carry on its restoration. Though work goes on, Larimer Square was a commercial success from the time its first shops and restaurants opened. Now listed in the National Register, and designated Denver's first historic preservation district, its popularity has made it a Denver landmark in more ways than one. A great deal of its success is due to careful supervision and quality control. Dana Crawford not only chooses Larimer Square tenants with care, she watches over them to make sure they maintain high standards, retaining approval of signs, graphics, and landscaping.

Another major attraction of the center is the expert fusing of Victorian buildings *(197, 198)* into an overall plan intermingling plazas, promenades, arches, and fountains *(194, 196)*. Two sunken central courtyards allow the use of basement space behind the buildings, on Larimer Lane *(195)*. Well-designed new construction melds with old sculpture and salvaged materials from the old Custom House, the Mining Exchange, and several Denver mansions. The resounding success of Larimer Square has helped awaken Denver's interest in its remaining early buildings; among those saved was the old Tramway Cable Building.

Built in 1889 by the Denver City Railway Company, the Tramway Cable Building *(200)* served the longest continuous cable system in the world at that time, supporting three separate lines totaling fifteen miles of track. Following the dramatic success of Larimer Square, this building, one of the few nineteenth-century structures remaining in the Skyline renewal area, was saved by newly founded Historic Denver, and declared a landmark by the Denver city

197

198

council. It now houses offices on the second floor and an antique shop and restaurant on the ground floor. The restaurant, a branch of a chain called The Old Spaghetti Factory that specializes in nostalgia, began attracting overflow crowds as soon as it opened. Another of the chain's eight restaurants is located in Salt Lake City's Trolley Square. All of the others occupy nineteenth-century buildings: an opera house in Tacoma, a bank in Spokane, and a pasta factory in San Jose, where the company helped launch a fund-raising drive for restoration of a nearby eighteenth-century adobe. The restaurant in the Tramway Cable Building features a wonderfully wild and whimsical assortment of nineteenth-century furnishings. Diners can eat at tables inside one of Denver's oldest trolleys *(color, page 222),* carefully restored and repainted in its original colors. Or they may choose from tables with seats made from the ends of bedsteads of all sorts: brass, iron, wood, and curtained fourposters. Tiffany glass and a variety of Victorian chandeliers hang from the high, rough wood beams of the original ceiling of the cable car barn. The bar *(199)* was brought by ship in the late 1880s to serve prospectors in a Nome, Alaska, saloon, and was later moved to the Barbary Coast Bar in Portland, Oregon, before it was installed here, flanked by an antique barber chair and an old Victrola. In keeping with the surroundings, the menu is decorated with ads reproduced from an 1897 mail-order catalogue showing stereopticons, tire benders, buggies, and assorted fashions.

201

Hotel: **Bank, Jacksonville, Oregon**

202

Jacksonville, founded in 1852 after the discovery of gold in southern Oregon, was a town of fifteen thousand people at its height. When the gold fever died down, Jacksonville evolved into a prosperous agricultural center, but its fortunes fell when it was bypassed by the railroad in 1883. Population dropped to one thousand, and the county seat was moved to Medford. Many Jacksonville residents survived the Depression by digging for gold in their backyards.

As in a number of other cities, poverty acted as a preservative, and Jacksonville remained a living reminder of the nineteenth century. However, in recent years, its citizens have had to fight to save its collection of downtown brick buildings and early residences. In 1962, there was a successful battle against a four-lane highway that would have cut through eight city blocks. Two years later the city council rejected an urban renewal plan for the downtown area.

The village, designated a Registered National Landmark in 1967, enacted a historic preservation ordinance. Its restoration became the responsibility of preservationists and private business. One of their first and most notable successes, as well as a fine example of preservation technique, is the restoration of the United States Hotel (201) and its conversion to a bank.

The hotel, built in 1880, boasted President Rutherford B. Hayes as one of its early guests. Taken over by the county for back taxes in 1915, it was used as a museum until 1949, when it was declared unsafe by public officials. Citizens saw their chance to save the condemned building by persuading the National Bank of Portland to adapt it for use as its new branch, rather than begin new construction on vacant land, for which it had an option.

A nonprofit corporation was formed to take over the building when the bank agreed to lease the ground floor. On the strength of the lease, $45,000 was borrowed, and with an additional prepayment of ten years' rent by the cooperative bank, restoration of the hotel could proceed.

Because of this beneficial cooperation, plus an advisory committee of experts meeting regularly with architect and building department, an important building in Jacksonville's nineteenth-century downtown has been saved, and the resulting banking office is authentic from its inkwells to its carved wooden fixtures (202).

Old City Hall: Restaurant and Offices, Boston, Massachusetts

Mayor Kevin White hailed it as "a successful effort to project an important political, architectural and historical landmark into a new century and a new use . . . proof that the preservation of our past is an ornament in our future." Ada Louise Huxtable announced, "The Old City Hall is alive and well and making money in Boston, offering elegant offices, French cuisine . . . and a landmark lesson in preservation and real estate development."

They said it couldn't be done, but the vision, determination, and pragmatism of a man named Roger Webb saved Boston's old City Hall (1862) for a productive new life. A blue-ribbon panel had recommended against preservation when the projected cost of saving the flamboyant French Second Empire building made its renovation appear impractical, following removal of government offices to new quarters. Webb, who had been in the business of moving old houses to new sites, undertook his own feasibility study, and came up with lower cost estimates

and a workable plan to put the building on a paying basis. Not without difficulty, he won the job of developing his plans, and carried them out through his newly formed nonprofit corporation, Architectural Heritage, Inc.

Surrounded by the severely simple towers of modern skyscrapers, which dwarf its ornate, sculptured mass, the old City Hall (205) contributes welcome variety and contrast to the city scene. Its interior space works aesthetically and efficiently. Upper floors accommodate handsome modern offices, with interior arches that repeat the window motif. Ironically, one of the offices is occupied by a company that worked in favor of demolishing the building.

One side of the first floor houses a bank; the other a French restaurant, Maison Robert (204). Monsieur Robert cautiously opened his restaurant in the vaulted brick cellar before committing himself to the grander rooms he had leased upstairs. With success assured, he called in interior designer Leslie Larson to make the

most of the beautiful, high-ceilinged rooms on the main floor. These rooms, retaining the only original woodwork left in the building, had served as a dumping ground for all the doors and paneling that had been stripped from other floors. Larson re-used the lovely old wood wherever possible, treating the inherent grandeur of the rooms with dignity and restraint (203).

Architectural Heritage oversees the maintenance of the building from its offices downstairs, while working on new plans and feasibility studies for adaptive use of buildings in Boston and elsewhere. Other cities with important old buildings that seem impossible to save are calling on Webb to devise practical adaptations that will work for their needs. In Boston, the firm has been working on the restoration and adaptive use of Quincy Market, where original storekeepers will be encouraged to return, while new boutiques and outdoor cafés on terraced malls will be added to existing facilities.

203

204

207

208

Trolley Barns: **Trolley Square, Salt Lake City, Utah**

Converting obsolete trolley barns into a lively, profitable entertainment and shopping complex is an example of preservation and adaptive use at its most imaginative. Built by railroad magnate E. H. Harriman, in 1908, on the site of Utah's Territorial Fairgrounds, the buildings housed Salt Lake City's trolleys until they were phased out in 1945. Buses that replaced the trolleys used the buildings until 1969, when the transit system relocated. Realtor Wallace A. Wright, Jr., conceived the idea of turning the thirteen acres and immense structures into an attractive commercial center, with a turn-of-the-century atmosphere. The five 420-foot-long bays, with 33-foot-high ceilings, form interconnecting, enclosed malls, their streets paved with old brick (209, 211). Layers of yellow paint were sand-blasted from the Mission-style brick façade, and forty antique cast-iron fixtures that used to light downtown Salt Lake City now illuminate Trolley Square at night (208). The building's 208 sky-lights were retained to provide daylight for the balconies and bays. Incorporated into the multi-level interior are the salvaged components of demolished Salt Lake City mansions, including dormer windows, doors, ornamental stairways, and a 28-foot stained-glass dome (206). The cupola of a Victorian mansion has been installed intact (207), and a handbag shop is housed in a stationary antique elevator cage (210). The 97-foot water tower, embellished with a spiral staircase, wrought-iron decoration, and six thousand lights, serves as an observation platform, and will eventually house a radio station. The old machine shop has become a theater, decorated with huge murals of former film stars, and the sand house now stores money for the First Security Bank. A restored trolley car, one of eleven old cars that were found and acquired by Mr. Wright, serves as a bank branch office (color, page 239). The cars were being used as chicken coops, motel units, and garages, and were in dreadful condition. After restoration, they were put into service for a variety of businesses: among them are a florist, a sporting-goods shop, and a restaurant. Trolley Square's carefully selected tenants include several theaters, numerous restaurants, sidewalk cafés, an ice-cream parlor, an endless variety of shops and boutiques, and an old-fashioned farmer's market.

206

211

Skid Row: **Pioneer Square, Seattle, Washington**

Seattle businessmen are finding that old buildings can be money-makers. In five years assessed valuation in the Pioneer Square district increased six hundred per cent; and while city building permits were down by six per cent, in Pioneer Square they increased eight hundred per cent! The enlightened policies of Mayor Wes Uhlman and his preservation-minded city council (which may well be the most forward-looking in the country) have had a great deal to do with this success by actively encouraging the private effort that had already begun reclaiming Seattle's oldest buildings from urban blight.

Pioneer Square, actually a triangle, was the city's original commercial district. It was known as skid road in the mid-nineteenth century when logs were skidded down to a sawmill on Puget Sound, but the area, which included the vice-ridden Tenderloin, was leveled by a major fire in 1889. Rebuilding in this enforced urban renewal was largely influenced by one architect, giving the district an unusual homogeneity. However, after 1910, the business center began to move northward, and from World War I onward, deterioration set in. The term skid road began to apply to the district in another sense— with the connotation that it has come to have in other American cities. Many of its buildings were vacant, and there were the familiar proposals for running a freeway through the middle of the area, as well as plans for urban renewal demolition.

Though some individual effort was initiated as early as 1954 toward resurrection of the area, effective change really began when Barbara Buck bought the small, triangular Baranof Hotel as headquarters for her magazine, *Pacific Banker and Business,* in 1967. In 1971, architect Ralph Anderson converted the Grand Central Hotel to the Grand Central Arcade *(color, page 240),* a multilevel complex of shops and offices. Also in 1971, the first bank opened in the area, and restaurants, sidewalk cafés, stores, and offices proliferated *(215).* Behind the arcade, in Occidental Park, lunch-hour crowds of office workers began watching strolling musicians and actors, buying from vendors of art, crafts, and food.

The eighteen square blocks were finally designated as the Pioneer Square historic district, and the city became the first to allot revenue-sharing funds to a restoration project, as $600,000 was allocated for a revolving fund to buy, rehabilitate, and resell historic buildings. Model Cities funding was used to enlarge and develop parks. In a reversal of traditional American policy favoring the automobile over the human being, streets were narrowed rather than widened, with a major avenue closed to traffic and

212

converted to a brick-paved mall. Lights and traffic signals are being replaced with reproductions of old ones, and old-fashioned street furniture and drinking fountains are being installed *(212, 213, 214)*.

Another major break-through is a minimum-maintenance ordinance requiring property owners to keep their buildings in good condition. Additionally, whenever the city needs new office space, top priority is given to locating in Pioneer Square. Businessmen are following; moving out of new skyscrapers into Pioneer Square.

215

Skid Row: **Pioneer Square, Seattle, Washington**

Organizations

This listing is organized alphabetically by city.

Historic Alexandria Foundation
P.O. Box 524
Alexandria, Virginia 22314

Historic Annapolis, Inc.
18 Pinkney Street
Annapolis, Maryland 21401

Tri-County Conservancy of the Brandywine, Inc.
P.O. Box 141
U.S. Route 1
Chadds Ford, Pennsylvania 19317

Historic Charleston Foundation
51 Meeting Street
Charleston, South Carolina 29401

Chicago School of Architecture Foundation
Glessner House
1800 South Prairie Avenue
Chicago, Illinois 60616

Lincoln Park Conservation Association
c/o Lawrence D. Glass
676 North LaSalle Street
Chicago, Illinois 60616

Historic Covington
c/o Charles Eilerman
22 Swain Court
Covington, Kentucky 41011

Historic Denver, Inc.
1340 Pennsylvania Street
Denver, Colorado 80203

Galena Historical Association
South Bench Street
Galena, Illinois 61036

Georgetown Historical Society, Inc.
P.O. Box 657
Georgetown, Colorado 80444

Old Island Restoration Foundation
P.O. Box 689
Old Mallory Square
Key West, Florida 33040

Marshall Historical Society
P.O. Box 15
Marshall, Michigan 49068

Mobile Historic Development Commission
P.O. Box 1827
City Hall
Mobile, Alabama 36601

Pilgrimage Garden Club
P.O. Box 237
Natchez, Mississippi 39120

Louisiana Landmarks Society
201 Gallier Hall
545 St. Charles Avenue
New Orleans, Louisiana 70130

Vieux Carré Property Owners and Associates
P.O. Box 2485
Custom House Station
New Orleans, Louisiana 70176

Brownstone Revival Committee
Room 1825
230 Park Avenue
New York, New York 10017

Oldport Association, Inc.
P.O. Box 238
Newport, Rhode Island 02840

Victorian Society
The Athenaeum
East Washington Square
Philadelphia, Pennsylvania 19106

Strawberry Banke, Inc.
P.O. Box 300
Hancock and Washington Streets
Portsmouth, New Hampshire 03801

Providence Preservation Society
24 Meeting Street
Providence, Rhode Island 02903

Historic Richmond Foundation
2407 East Grace Street
Richmond, Virginia 23223

Lafayette Square Restoration Committee
P.O. Box 7215
St. Louis, Missouri

Foundation for the Restoration of Ste. Genevieve
34 South 3d Street
Ste. Genevieve, Missouri 63670

San Antonio Conservation Society
511 Paseo de la Villita
San Antonio, Texas 78205

Foundation for San Francisco's Architectural
   Heritage
P.O. Box 2379
2007 Franklin Street
San Francisco, California 94109

San Francisco Victoriana
606 Natoma Street
San Francisco, California 94103

Victorian Alliance
4143 23d Street
San Francisco, California 94114

Old Santa Fe Association, Inc.
545 Canyon Road
Santa Fe, New Mexico 87501

Historic Savannah Foundation
119 Habersham Street
Savannah, Georgia 31402

Stockade Association
c/o Jacob Schmitt
217 Union Street
Schenectady, New York 12305

National Trust for Historic Preservation
740-748 Jackson Place, N.W.
Washington, D.C. 20006

Old Salem, Inc.
P.O. Drawer F
Salem Station
Winston-Salem, North Carolina 27108